THE TEARS OF EROS

THE TEARS OF EROS

by Georges Bataille

Translated by Peter Connor

City Lights Books

San Francisco

This book was originally published as *Les larmes d'Eros*, © 1961 by Jacques Pauvert, Paris

The Tears of Eros was published in several versions in France after the original Pauvert edition. This first English language translation includes most of the illustrations which appear in the original.

Cover design: Rex Ray

Library of Congress Cataloging-in-Publication Data

Bataille, Georges. 1897-1962
   [Larmes d'Eros. English]
   The tears of Eros / by Georges Bataille: translated
  by Peter Connor.
    p. 224
   Translation of: Les larmes d'Eros.
   ISBN 0-87286-222-4 (pbk) : $14.95
   1. Erotic Art. I. Title.
  N8217.E6B313   1988   88-16164
  704.9'428--dc19   CIP

Printed in Hong Kong

City Lights Books are available to bookstores through our primary distributor: Subterranean Company, P.O. Box 10233, Eugene, OR 97440. (800) 274-7826. Our books are also available through library jobbers and regional distributors. For personal orders and catalogs, please write to City Lights Mail Order: 261 Columbus Avenue, San Francisco, CA 94133.

CITY LIGHTS BOOKS are edited by Lawrence Ferlinghtetti & Nancy J. Peters and published at the City Lights Bookstore, 261 Columbus Avenue, San Francisco, California 94133.

CONTENTS

Georges Bataille, From Afar . . ., An Introduction by J.M. Lo Duca   1

Letters   9

Foreword by Georges Bataille   19

Part One: The Beginning (The Birth of Eros)
I. THE CONSCIOUSNESS OF DEATH
1. Eroticism, Death and the 'Devil'   23
2. Prehistoric Man and the Painted Caves   25
3. Eroticism Linked to the Awareness of Death   32
4. Death at the Bottom of the 'Pit' in the Lascaux Cave   34

II. WORK AND PLAY
1. Eroticism, Work and the 'Little Death'   39
2. Doubly Magical Caves   45

Part Two: The End (From Antiquity to the Present Day)
I. DIONYSOS OR ANTIQUITY
1. The Birth of War   57
2. Slavery and Prostitution   58
3. The Primacy of Work   60
4. On the Role of the Lower Classes in the Development of Religious Eroticism   64
5. From Erotic Laughter to Prohibition   66
6. Tragic Eroticism   69
7. The God of Transgression and the Feast: Dionysos   70
8. The Dionysiac World   72

II. THE CHRISTIAN ERA
1. From Christian Condemnation to Morbid Exaltation
   (Or from Christianity to Satanism)   79
2. The Reappearance of Eroticism in Painting   82
3. Mannerism   87
4. Libertinage in the Eighteenth Century and the Marquis de Sade   103
5. Goya   129
6. Gilles de Rais and Erzsébet Báthory   138

7. The Evolution of the Modern World   142
8. Delacroix, Manet, Degas, Gustave Moreau and the Surrealists   152

III. BY WAY OF CONCLUSION

1. Compelling Figures   162
2. Voodoo Sacrifice   199
3. Chinese Torture   205

GEORGES BATAILLE, FROM AFAR . . .

I. Who speaks here? The witness, the critic, the collaborator, the historian, the friend? Each one would need more than a year to sketch out a serious discourse, or to act as a disciple and remain silent. Even at the outer edges of intuition I can do no more than cast a glance, in broad daylight, into the night of this new Plato's cave which Georges Bataille has hollowed out in order to think through the darkness of the unspeakable.

The witness proves, however, unexpectedly helpful. In Bataille there was a man—a very beautiful and very saintly man—and to have seen him live cannot but scatter sparks of light into the darkness of his work. Paul Valéry himself deemed it fitting to follow, line by line, image by image, caption by caption, the making of an entire book by this infinitely peaceable author who was so haunted by its destiny. It is thus that I see the gentle historian moving across the highly waxed floor of the Bibliothèque d'Orléans, or among the blue and gold bookcases of what used to be the palace of the archbishop of that town. This makes it easier for me to open the briefcase in which fifty-seven of his letters (some of them six pages long) still speak of the slow pace of writing, of concern over the illustrations for a thesis on eroticism that has become, through force of time, his last will and testament. I admit it: I am proud to have been at that particular moment at the heart of the personal history of Georges Bataille.

These letters are from Orléans, of course, from Fontenay-le-Conte, from Sables d'Olonne, from Seillans and from Vézelay. I have also copied, by hand on two fragments of orange paper, the text by Georges Dumas on *Pleasure and Pain*, which so impressed him. And his notes, the foreword (nine manuscript sheets), and the first meticulously corrected proofs. And also a letter from Henri Parisot, which filled him with joy, accompanying the color photograph of Balthus' *The Guitar Lesson* (it was around the time of the *Méthode de Méditation*).

It was on the 24th of July, 1959, that Bataille decided upon the title of this book: *The Tears of Eros* ("Pauvert will love it," he added, not without malice). On the same date, he asked me in regard to the *New Dictionary of Sexology* to make sure to include articles on Gilles de Rais, Erzsébet Báthory, the Sacred, Transgression, Fashion, Nudity, Jean Genet, Pierre Klossowski . . . his favorite voices.

The idea of *The Tears of Eros* never left him, and he planned it down to the most minute detail, from the economy of the chapters to the cropping of the photographs (he even made me a sketch of a tapestry by Rosso in which I was supposed to find a detail which interested him), and including a very elaborate selection of images from the prehistoric era, the Ecole de Fontainebleau, and from the Surrealists, both avowed and clandestine.

For two years, from July, 1959 to April, 1961, he elaborated the layout of this work, which increasingly took on the proportions of a conclusion to all the themes he had loved. Putting it together, however, was slow, and *The Tears of Eros* was held up both by circumstance ["Meanwhile, my eldest daughter has been arrested for her activities (for Algeria)"[1]] and by the decline of his physical strength (". . . I must admit, I am not seeing very clearly. . . . ").[2] The book was finished—I shall say later under what circumstances—and he was happy with it: it was a unified whole, from the choice of the typeface to the rhythm of the page layouts; he had taken care that his ideas were neither slowed down, nor impeded, nor betrayed by a misplaced image. Although he was the most courteous of men, Bataille became peremptory when it came to supervising the material form his work should take.[3] *The Tears of Eros* was well done indeed, and Bataille had in a sense been able to fulfill the desire of Valéry, for whom an image could often advantageously replace a writer's fallacious description. From Gautier d'Agoty to the plates by Cranach and to Christian and Chinese tortures, the image *said* everything in a compressed form, whereas words were only a tame reflection. The book pleased him and I presume it must have brought him one of his last joys. He never had the annoyance of knowing about the blacklisting of his book by our deplorable censor—Malraux was in power—on one of his most ignoble days, one in the sequence that saw him make the mistake of banning Stekel, Havelock Ellis and Alban Berg. Bataille was by then beyond reach. The act of censorship revelled only in its own shame (along with the whole[4] of the French press, it might be said in passing, who remained silent).

II. My relationship with Georges Bataille and the context of this book—which he wrote during this time—contribute to the delineation of my hypothesis: very early on, Georges Bataille must have abandoned himself to the anguish of death, perhaps even to an inner panic that ended in a system of defense; his entire work is laid out over this defensive mask. In order to tolerate the idea of death in these conditions, it had to be at one and the same time dressed up in sparkling colors, reduced to a sublime moment (*the last moment*), laughed at, and made into "the most horrible of horrible things," "the single harbour against the torments of this life."[5] Finally, there is the trace of that wild desire to avert its impact by refusing to draw a conlcusion. "These judgments should lead to silence and I write. This is in no way paradoxical." Yes, but to express silence, silence no longer suffices. Others have tried the absolute renunciation of writing. They make me think irresistibly of a sentence in Chateaubriand (addressed to Julia Michel in 1838): "I am an enemy of every book, and if I could destroy my own, I would not fail to do so." Even the *Mémoires d'Outre-Tombe* is virtually finished. Language may indeed be an obstacle, but it is also the *only* means.

"You will hear, coming from within, a voice that leads to your destiny. It is the voice of desire, and not that of any desirable being." Here again we find Bataille's incisive poetry, without literary resonance, as when he states: "The wind from outside is writing this book." He must have been aware of how much the proclaimed impersonality of thinking in reality bears *his* signature. Whether he likes it or not, it is Hegel who suggests to him that "the life that withstands death and sustains itself in it is the life of the mind" (I quote from memory). This is what marks the superiority of Hegelian thought, which is composed of knowing *and* knowledge, over other currents of thought, which have only knowing, and which for this very reason are blind.

Hegel makes his brief entrance here. It is not that we want at all costs to link Hegel to Bataille. The spiraling depths of his thought are such that we might find in the creator of *Acéphale* other masters, and even Heraclitus would be appropriate here, from the child's game of gathering stones to build castles only to destroy them, sometimes even with the complicity of the tide, to creation by fire. We could also seek an ancestor for each of his rational or irrational remarks. Whence comes the gratuitousness of human activity, its enormous waste—two hundred million eggs for a single mortal being—its taste for rebirth at the price of a destructive act? Whence Bataille's fundamental insight—which in fact owes nothing to ethnology nor to Marcel Griaule—that *Homo sapiens* arrives at consciousness through his erect sex? Whence stems this tendency to translate religious anxiety into sexual obsession? Whence the obvious idea that "sovereign, absolute liberty was foreseen [. . .] after the revolutionary negation of the principle of royalty?"

This would be a game—not to be disdained—that remains outside of our interests here.

III. More memories, weaving their way into my discussion. Orléans. Last phase of *The Tears of Eros*. There is in this town a very tall, narrow house, with a white marble façade in the style of the late Renaissance. Today it is only a warehouse for innumerable cheeses, and this you can tell even from the middle of the marketplace facing it. Georges Bataille was fascinated by the whole scene and by the incongruity of this cheese company's architecture. Amazing correspondences must also have been springing up in his mind. I was able to judge this objectively in spite of my own hatred of the smell of cheese. Amid this ornate marble, then, Bataille and Monique laid in ample provisions for lunch on the day he was finally finishing *The Tears of Eros*. Monique, moreover, outdid him on his home ground, sampling a cheese compared to which Munster smells like a violet, a cheese before which even he had hesitated. His eyes bright with admiration, he murmured: "It's almost a tomb."

From these gustatory and olfactory pleasures he no doubt drew—not forgetting his trouble with recall—renewed strength for the finishing touches of what would be this book. For months I suffered Monique's reproaches for what she called my cruelty. And it was indeed cruelty. To the extent that he was capable, I made him write the captions that he wanted to see throughout *The Tears of Eros*. As soon as the caption was written, in his steady handwriting, minute and precise, he took it into the next room, where Monique would type it. At this point Bataille's fatigue was so great, his concentration had produced such a consuming tenseness, that when I came back he had already forgotten what he had just written.

Nevertheless, I had to finish this book, which had taken a year longer than the editor had planned. This is my only excuse, and it does not stop my heart from tightening whenever I think that I could have prevented his suffering by giving up the book and leaving intact the immemorial taboos that he wanted to shatter at all costs.

I also discover Georges Bataille in an old essay, of which I have a reprint from "Aréthuse," entitled *Coins of the Great Moguls.*[6] Already the stamp of the writer and thinker is felt in this somewhat routine cultural exercise. From the empire "of such an abruptly dazzling destiny" of the nephew of Tamerlane, Babar, descended from Gengis Khan by his mother, to the Jesuits deluding themselves "with foolish hopes of the imminent conversion . . . of India," Georges Bataille displays his personal vision of the world of history. And all this in a catalogue of zodiacal coins!

However, if a style of writing was already manifest, his thought had not yet revealed itself. The relationship between eroticism and death still remains in the very texture of human activity and if it surfaces in his mind, it remains unformulated. He is in any case in good company. Georges Bernanos wrote, "It surely seems that the presentiment of death determines our affective life."[7]

Georges Bataille can indeed easily turn to the Orient to find other strata of this unchanging concept. There is Nirvana and maithuna (sexual union), which are opposed to the nonhuman type of "heavenly" thought. In fact, Nirvana is at the same time the death of the Buddha, the annihilation of physical life, and the "little death,"* so dear to Bataille. He was a convinced Hegelian; however, Schopenhauer did not displease him. It is to the latter that we owe the diffusion of this term in the West, in the sense of the extinction of desire, the annihilation of the individual in the collective, a state of tranquility, therefore of perfect happiness, *where death no longer has any meaning,* something that leaves Bataille overwhelmed with fear. Freud sees in it an "effort to reduce, to keep constant or to remove internal tension."[8] Thus he discerns in it a correspondence with the notion of the death drive.[9] We cannot ignore his remarks.

On a level much closer to the poetry of Bataille, Novalis—the great Novalis to whom we must turn each time a haunting intuition arises in our minds—has also said: "The process of history is a blazing fire, and death can represent the positive limit of the transcendence of a life beyond life."

Georges Bataille in fact does not so much turn his gaze toward death as toward the *last instant,* that last instant in which one must shatter the powers of eternity. From elimination to elimination, pain appears to him as a mediator—an intermediary and go-between—between life and death. Hence his gaze is fixed—Max von Sydow has just this gaze when he tries to penetrate the eyes of a woman who is about to be burned (*The Seventh Seal*)—on torture victims. Here we should also recall that one of the founding doctrines of the Buddha is the truth of pain, where masochistic acceptance and sadistic provocation are closely linked. One might recall this sentence which Bataille writes elsewhere: "Often Hegel seems to me quite obvious, but this obviousness is a heavy burden."[10] The obviousness of the links that lead to the *last instant* must be just as heavy to bear. This last instant will be a leitmotif engraved throughout his work, probably with the help of Nietzsche's cautery.

It is this *last instant* which drives Bataille to search for *proofs.* His intuition—nourished also by Hegel, Nietzsche and Freud—admits with ease that "it is the sexual instincts . . . which in the end explain the horrors of sacrifice."[11] He knows only too well that the pleasure of going beyond oneself through self-annihilation is a sadistic pleasure par excellence. But this is not the object of his search. He would like to know *how* to reach the mediating point between sacrifice and ecstasy. The *why* is of little importance to him.

In the Chinese torture of a hundred pieces,[12] he is drawn toward the sight of a transfigured, ecstatic man under the knife of an executioner who is cutting him up alive, much to the joy of the onlookers. Bataille was not disturbed by the fact that the snapshot captured only an ephemeral fraction of the victim's expression and that, in any case, in the hands of a facetious medical student a corpse can be made to laugh by manipulating the orbicular of the lips; nor did knowing that the torture victim had received a strong dose of opium sow even a seed of doubt in him. The victims and the executioners convinced him that the mystery of the *last instant* is in this supreme anguish which, being *beyond,* must be resolved in supreme pleasure or in a supreme loss of consciousness. Bataille knew of the frenetic rites of the disciples of the Roufai, an Islamic sect linked to the Sufism of the dervishes, in which the pain of wounds incurred is used as a kind of ecstatic accompaniment (but "they are made in a state of such inner strength that they do not cause *pain* but a kind of beatitude which is an exaltation of the body as much as of the soul [. . .]. These practices should be considered above all as a means of opening a door.")[13]

This is the greatness and the weakness of the proof: for pain not to be pain, for death not to be the horror of death, they must stop short of becoming realities.

In Bataille's mythology, the ecstasy of the torture victim lent weight to the ecstasy of the great sadists—Gilles de Rais, Erzsébet Báthory de Nassady, Doña Catalina de los Rios (whom Bataille did not have time to get to know)—or again to the man who *wanted* to see the tortured bodies of which Plato speaks,[14] to the ithyphallic flagellators of Christ as witnessed in traditional paintings and sculptures (Luis Borrasà, Holbein, the Breton Calvaries), in short to the permanent taste of the crowd for the most cruel spectacles of death—the Circus, the Crucifixion, Tenochtitlan, Place de Grève, Red Square, or Nuremburg. Everything takes on meaning, but only in the direction of destruction and death. Schlegel said, "It is only in the enthusiasm of destruction that the meaning of divine creation is revealed. It is only in the midst of death that eternal life flares up."[15] Which is not far from Hegel's "Liberty, terror, and death are linked."

To question suffering is then simply a way of approaching the question of death. Georges Bataille's touching attempts cannot cross the frontier of the unknowable. It is already very fine that he was able to reconcile himself to the dialectic expressed in the concept of *Aufheben* (to negate while at the same time preserving)—particularly dear to a Hegelian mind—by consenting to survive and thus to write. The "write with your blood" of Nietzsche sometimes becomes in him "write with your life," "write as you laugh" (*On Nietzsche*).

IV. Even the most casual reader will have noticed: I am sidestepping something. I have resisted with all my strength the idea of speaking of Bataille on any other level. I have been delaying this moment, and although I am reluctant to give him the name of philosopher, I must now forget his poetic language, which I always found more compelling, so as to speak of the way he thinks. I approach the philosopher with all the reservations philosophy has taught me. I have said elsewhere that we are living with a twenty-five-hundred-year-old discourse, that we call "philosophy" precisely for want of a more uncertain word. We have been guilty enough to forget that its birth was conditioned by myth, religion, even politics, which means that it is the only domain in which we have accepted supposition, in an area where science had always demanded description.

Philosophy has been a concave or convex mirror that man has constructed for himself (without admitting it) to make us see how *we should have been,* and not at all to show us how we are.[16]

The polluted philosophies of Christianity tried hard to separate Life from the activity of the endocrine glands; but they are no worse than the secular philosophies, which separate man from his, let us say, excremental activities. This makes us think of those sublime architects who nonetheless forget that in a kitchen it sometimes happens that water boils. . . .

Georges Bataille should really be approached between Hegel and Nietzche, between the dialectic and the tragic. His definitive and radical experience of "the impossibility of thinking"—expressed moreover in a sustained current of thought that surges continuously through his works—will not stop us or hinder us from seeing this experience distinctly, in spite of the difficulties his research takes pleasure in engendering. "Experience is an authority unto itself, but [. . .] an authority in atonement."[17] He is trying to define, I think, the principle of an "intellectual" life free from any authority which would be the source of a thinking-that-has-no-source. But Bataille ends by expressing the limits which are our own, because what he fears—the betrayal of speech—is already inscribed in the originary articulation of speech. When he says: "A man is a particle *inserted* into unstable and entangled wholes," this *inserted* compromises forever all hope of absence.

We cannot, or not without falling into the void, get around these security devices; by reversing them—by sophistry or by a prodigious *élan*—it is perhaps possible to attain to *atheology,* but we then just as surely dissolve in the absence of the divine and the ego which is in the end simply absence. But how can one close one's eyes to this absence which, in order to be intelligible, is within a presence? It is moreover only the atheists who dramatize the absence of God; for the others, it is an unbounded relief.

Should we invoke Freud? Perhaps the key—or the catch—to this anxiety is in his hands. His early statement that "anxiety is the result of a repression" certainly doesn't help us any, even if we analyze Georges Bataille's memories about his father. What has an altogether different importance is the certainty that "the ultimate transformation of anxiety is the anxiety of death, fear in front of the superego projected onto the power of destiny."[18]

A former analysand (word has it that Lacan never allowed himself to be analyzed by any of his colleagues) knows all the nuances of the death drive (*Todestriebe*), the extreme impulses that are opposed to the life drive and tend to the complete resolution of tensions, that is to say, they tend to bring the living being back to an inorganic state.[19] There is a fundamental tendency in every living being to return to this state. And the rest follows with a kind of fatalism: "A portion of this drive leads to sadism by being diverted outwards (towards objects in the external world); the portion that does not share in this displacement outwards remains inside the organism, where it becomes libidinally bound. It is in this portion that we recognize the original, erotogenic masochism."[20]

Almost everything is said, and if we add Freud's thinking to what must have been, in Bataille's mind, a meditation on the *last instant,* we gain some clarity: "When there is physical pain, a high degree of what may be termed narcissistic cathexis of the painful place occurs; this cathexis continues to increase and tends, as it were, to 'empty' the ego."[21]

This kind of cross-checking can go pretty far. One can rightly ask if a haunting fear of death did not leave Georges Bataille struck with astonishment. "No more than upon the sun can the gaze rest upon death."[22] Could this be any closer to the symbolism that taught us about "the close likeness of beauty and death"?[23]

I am more at ease with Georges Bataille the astonished poet, one whose style is nonetheless already thought through and who, simply by entering into the universe of words and forms, belies the atrocity he tried to circumvent in order to attenuate the supreme atrocity of nonbeing. He does not answer Valéry's question: "Why does that which creates living beings, create them mortal?"[24] for the excellent reason that the answer will always evade us as long as we do not go beyond life.

V. I last saw Bataille sitting at the Café de Flore one sunny morning. Around him (it was perhaps the last time they were to meet) is Balthus, and beside Balthus is Pierre Klossowski, two sides of the same medallion. A little further away, Patrick Waldberg, as attentive as a nurse. Georges Bataille is there, blue eyes, white hair, and incomparably youthful. A silence descended as though an angel were passing. I never saw him again, and so he remains in the morning sun, he who dreamed only of doveless tombs.

J. M. Lo Duca

1. 15 June 1960.
2. 21 February 1961.
3. "... [Capuletti is placed] in the middle of the horrors and the tortures, which cannot be interrupted in this way. This absolutely disrupts the logic of these illustrations [...] you must find a way to put the Capuletti before the sequence on 'voodoo sacrifice' [...] It bothers me to have to demand something so categorically ... " Orléans, 22 May 1961.
4. I mean and I write *the whole.*
5. Montaigne, *Essais,* I, XIV.
6. No. 13–14, October 1926–January 1927.
7. *Les grands cimetières sous la lune.* Quoted by Michel Sorel: *Homoeroticus in Frankreich* (Munich: Verlag Kurt Desch).
8. *Beyond the Pleasure Principle,* in *The Standard Edition of the Complete Psychological Works of Sigmund Freud* (London: Hogarth, 1953–74), vol. 18, p. 55.
9. *S.E.,* vol. 19, p. 160.
10. Georges Bataille, *Guilty,* trans. Bruce Boone (Venice, CA: Lapis, 1988).
11. In the monumental preface to *Justine* (Paris: J. J. Pauvert, 1956).
12. This torture must have haunted Paris from 1913 to 1918 (and there were plenty of Western examples of it!). It has been vulgarized, if I may say so, by a certain Louis Carpeaux in a book that one used to find at the bedside of the great actresses: *Pékin s'en va* (1913); it is the "dismemberment of Fou-Tchou-Li" (a series of Verascope photographs which one sees everywhere nowadays).

13. *Introduzione alla Magia quale scienza dell'Io,* by the "Groupe d'Ur" (Rome: vol. 11, p. 204.)
14. *On Justice,* IV.
15. Schlegel, *Ideen,* Minor, no. 131.
16. *Erotique de l'Art,* vol. 36, p. 531.
17. Georges Bataille, *Inner Experience,* trans. Leslie Anne Boldt (New York: SUNY Press, 1988). Cf. Maurice Blanchot, *Faux pas* (Paris: Gallimard, 1943), pp. 47–52.
18. Nunberg.
19. *Beyond the Pleasure Principle, SE,* vol. 18, p. 50.
20. *The Economic Problem of Masochism, SE,* vol. 19, p. 164.
21. *Inhibition, Symptom and Anxiety, SE,* vol. 20, p. 171. With regard to Freud, Bataille used to smile at the cultural pretensions of Paris, where Freud's complete works were not yet available (nor, at the time, were those of Marx).
22. La Rochefoucauld.
23. J. P. Sartre.
24. Valéry, *Suite,* p. 139.

*See note, p. 34.

LETTERS*

Les Sables d'Olonne, 24 July 1959

My dear friend,

I have been meaning to write to you since July 10th. But my time has been taken up with the urgent need to get some texts sent off. And in any case I couldn't write to you until a good while after having received my notes. The second, and the last, of these texts finally went off yesterday. Since then I have been able to prepare this answer which has in its turn become urgent. . . .

I was delighted by what you wrote to me regarding the Institute for Sex Research at the University of Indiana. I am anxious to see you again, and I'm sure that we will have an important conversation, among other things about the illustrations for my book.

I have been able to bring into focus my plans and my notes for the possible illustrations.

I have in any case secured photographs of the remarkable scenes from Renais' film on Hiroshima, which will go well with the conclusion of the book. I would like to do a first part on Eros and cruelty, where I will speak about Gilles de Rais, about whom I can give some information, about Erszébet Bathory, whose crimes are no less horrifying, and about a young American criminal called William Heirens (these last two are unknown in France) who is of exceptional interest. Perhaps you would be better able than I to write to America for one or two photographs and perhaps some details about Heirens' history. (I only have one fairly well documented book, but it's always good to add more.)

* Some of the fifty-seven letters in the possession of J. M. Lo Duca.

9

The second part will center on beauty and will begin with a study of the sexual attraction of beauty in the prehistoric period (it is already essentially finished), and it could of course be illustrated. I already have some notes, which could certainly be augmented (but perhaps we should talk about this).

As soon as possible I will go to see Brassaï, who in my view is the best photographer of semi-nudes. We have been friends for a long time and I'll try to get as much as I can from him.

Aside from photographs of women, he has some fine photographs of obscene graffiti, and according to the last conversation I had with Pauvert, I have the impression that we can plan on publishing them. The would certainly go well with my text.

Needless to say, I am most interested in what you told me about the dictionary.* I have for some time now already been noting down the words that I would suggest to you, even though, for some of them, you might want to contact someone other than myself.

In any case, here is the list:

Gilles de Rais
Erzsébet Báthory
Heirens (William)
The Sacred
Transgression
Prehistory
Fashion
Nudity

Breaking and entering
Genet (Jean)
Klossowski (Pierre)
Douassot (Jean)

It would be very possible to augment this list considerably.

As for Jean Genet, I think that Patrick Waldberg could do a very good article. He could do another very good article on:

Modern painting

Needless to say, in fact, we have a lot to talk about. But I won't be in Paris before September. I am staying at Sables d'Olonnes, 17 quai Clemenceau, until the thirtieth. It looks like I'll spend the month of August in Vézelay, which is all the address you need. If you should be passing through . . . In any case you can telephone me in Vézelay, number 36 (they will come and get me, it only takes a moment).

Kindest regards,

G. B.

[P.S.] It now seems to me that the best title for my book is *Les Larmes d'Eros*. Pauvert will love it.

Orléans, 17 November 1959

My dear friend,

I am now back in Orléans. And if, as Pauvert tells me, you are planning to come to Orléans,

---

Cf. Nouveau Dictionnaire de Sexologie (Paris: Editions J.J. Pauvert, 1965).

I would be absolutely delighted to see you. I have been seriously preparing, and have even begun, my work, but what is needed now is to give the project a general focus. And I think we will have a long and, I'm sure, very interesting conversation. Could you call me at Orléans, 87–31–23. You can call direct, but I can't remember the number you have to begin with to get Orléans so I'm afraid you'll have to ask information.

So, à bientôt, I hope, with my warmest regards,

G. B.

Fontenay-le-Comte, 5 March 1960

My dear friend.

I must have appeared, from my last letter, in a very bad state. As far as the suffering goes, indeed you are not wrong. But there is no question of my neglecting anything regarding *Les Larmes d'Eros*. In particular, I wanted to talk to you today about the idea of giving a lecture when the book comes out. Regarding the subject of this lecture, I'll try to arrange it with André Breton.

But before I do that, I'd like to arrange with you some kind of schedule regarding the date for giving you the manuscript and a date for the appearance of the book.

At this point I can only speak theoretically. It's up to you to let me know, in agreement with Pauvert, the dates that seem possible to you.

Perhaps this would need to be arranged with Julliard as well.

The state of my health remains troubling, though the treatment I am following allows me to expect some improvement, and I have already regained a regular if slow work pattern.

Here's what I can tell you as of now: I have been able to rework the layout of my book so as to give it a more meaningful development, a more essential thrust. I would like to make it a more remarkable book than any of the ones I have already published.

Of course, it's up to me to name the date I'll give you the manuscript, and you can only agree to it. I suggest the early part of April, the fifth at the latest. I am taking into account the relative slowness of my work at present. In principle I should finish by March 31st, but a reprieve until April 5th seems prudent to me. March 31st is a Thursday, April 5th a Tuesday. I would ask you to think in particular about the publication date. This way I can, insofar as possible, make it coincide with the date of my lecture. If need be, it seems to me that it would be possible to organize this lecture perhaps with you and Patrick Waldberg, without having to turn to any established institutions. Let me know what you think of this. It is of course still very early, but I think it's prudent to plan everything in advance.

I would ask you to answer by return mail, if only to give me your agreement so that I can telephone you on Thursday morning,

March 10th, with a view to fixing the dates, at least provisionally.

Kindest regards,

G. B.

Orléans, 15 June 1960.

My dear friend,

I have just returned from Paris, where I tried to get you on the telephone. I suppose that if I had telephoned you on Monday or Tuesday I would have reached you, but as it happened I was overwhelmed by numerous rendez-vous.

In any case this letter will bring you up to date on my work. This has not been very extensive since we saw each other, my health has been worse and worse. Meanwhile my eldest daughter was arrested for political activities (for Algeria). In fact it was only on Saturday or Sunday that suddenly I reached a kind of threshold and I regained a normal state of health. I suggest that we meet on Sunday, the 26th or Monday, the 27th of June in Paris. I think that by that point, we will be in a position to prepare everything. Let me know if need be what you want most immediately, if you think the date is a little far off.
I think I can get the manuscript finished by the end of the month of July. I have to spend July in Sables d'Olonnes, where I will be well set up to work.

I am aware of my deficiencies over the last

months, but I think I can assure you of this: everything should be finished by July 31st. Of course the list of illustrations should be done earlier, and except for some *unforeseeable* event, we should come to the end towards the 26th of June [. . .].

G. B.

Les Sables d'Olonne, 13 July 1960

My dear friend,

What you say in your letter of the 11th seems very interesting. And I am happy that you already have the ektachrome.
I think that the black background of the cover will be enough to bring out the color.

I also bring to your attention right away a painting; I think a photograph of it would be highly desirable [. . .] I refer to the *Massacre of the Innocents** by Cornelis Cornelisz of Haarlem. It is cited by Leymarie, in his *Dutch Painting* [. . .] in terms that clarify the meaning for us.[. . .]

Aside from that I can promise you that I have seven photographs, five of which are of flagellation (they come from Seabrook). They are authentic. But we cannot give a more precise reference. This is a guaranteed promise.
This evening I'll try to give you the continuation of my list of yesterday, but it's not sure that these will be the last. In any case I'll give you the references right away for the Dutch books you lent me.[. . .]

Apart from this, I think you are in possession of the photographs made from the work by Fuchs that you lent me.

Kindest regards,

G. B.

[P.S.] You must [. . .] have the photographs by Pierre Verger which represent scenes from a sacrifice in Brazil. I lent them to you [. . .] one day at the at the Café Flore.

Finally, something very important: it would be very good if you were to go *on my behalf* to see Brassaï, one of the most remarkable living photographers (one of two or three), and who is moreover interested, to a certain degree, in the things we are interested in. He is the creator of the photographs that I sent to Girodias while he was alive, notably some photographs of graffiti. He should also have a photograph* of the famous phallus of Delos (of which I gave only a very poor reproduction in my *Erotism*).

developments I had foreseen and to leave intact only three parts: one on prehistory, another on Dionysianism, which is followed by what I call the modern experts on Dionysianism, including a brief survey of (witches') sabbaths at the end of the Middle Ages, and some contemporary Moslem sects. The third part should be a study of a modern aspect of eroticism, represented at the same time by Goya and Sade and which should be accompanied by a general piece on modern painting. I think I can assure you that this time it will be a well balanced work whose final form, after some relatively minor work, will now be most meaningful.

But I still have to ask you if we could meet, either in Paris or in Orléans, towards the 20th of September, so as to arrange everything that remains to be arranged. This done, the manuscript in its final stages should be given to the printer very early in October.

Kindest regards,

G. B.

Les Sables d'Olonne, 5 September 1960

My dear friend,

Although I have spent a few days in poor health, I nevertheless worked. I don't think I can explain to you in writing the kinds of difficulties I am coming across. Nor can I tell you the reasons which led me to suppress certain

Les Sables d'Olonne (undated)

My dear friend,

I have made and I am continuing to make a desperate effort to finish. Alas, the treatment I followed on the advice of my doctor to get back on my feet ended up having the opposite effect. I have no strength left. In spite of everything I am working, but I am progressing

* A photograph taken by Bataille himself.

very slowly, very, very slowly. I don't know what else to tell you. It sometimes even happens that I find myself looking at corrections which have made my text worse. Thank God, this isn't so on the whole, but it depicts a difficulty so great that only speaking with you would allow me to tell you of the state I am in.

The only thing I can say is that, on the one hand, I will do everything to get my nerves back in order at the level of medical treatments, and that on the other hand, I only stop working whenever it becomes apparent that the work is getting confused.

Don't abandon me. Write to me. Tell me how far along you are, exactly what you have in mind regarding the illustrations.

Above all, answer me on this particular point: until what date will you be in Paris, in other words, until what date can I try to meet you there.

I must excuse myself for all these difficulties and I ask you, in spite of it all, to count on me. In spite of everything, the work that remains for me to do is not such that I could think for a moment of slacking until the day I send you the finished manuscript; I am putting off everything else until that day.

Kindest regards,

G. B.

[P.S.] I definitely think that it would be very advantageous for us to meet. I'll do my best to

have typed up, some day soon, what there is in its final form.

Fontenay-le-Comte, 1 September 1960

My dear friend,

I am having very bad bouts of depression. They are thankfully brief. It's been bad these last few days, but I have been able to get back to work. I won't write any more to you today but I am leaving for Les Sables where I will be better accommodated; I'll write to you from there (same address as a month ago) tomorrow.

Kindest regards,

G. B.

I have reason to be [the letter is interrupted]

Orléans, 16 December 1960

My dear friend,

I am getting close to the end of my book. I have been working hard all this time. In any case the documentary part is complete. I have only to finish writing the text. And in general, it's going fairly well.

I will go to Paris either sometime next week after Christmas or else on New Year's Day (in which case I'll stay on for a few days).

Tell me if you are planning to be away, and on which dates. In fact, we should use this moment to settle everything concerning the illustrations.

In principle, if my health holds up the way it is doing at the moment—even if only just—but in spite of everything holds up, I think the book should be one of the best I have written, and at the same time one of the most accessible.

I don't dare speak to you about the date. I absolutely want to have finished by the end of the year. And with fifteen days left, I think I'll make it.

Tell me what date I might suggest a meeting with you.

Kindest regards,

G. B.

Fontenay-le-Comte, 23 February 1961

My dear friend,

I'll be expecting you Tuesday at Niort, at the train which is supposed to arrive at about one o'clock in the afternoon.

I am struggling along with great difficulty. But if on Monday I realize that I am not going to be able to make it, I'll telegraph you. Unfortunately, I feel pretty unwell today. But unless I telegraph you tomorrow, this will probably mean that my health has picked up again. Moreover if I don't telegraph, I'll write, and you should have my letter by Monday morning.

But if you need to telephone me, you can call me.[. . .]

I'm having some difficulty, but all in all it seems to me unlikely that I won't get to the end. . . .

Warmest regards,

G. B.

Fontenay, 1 March 1961

My dear friend,

I was most happy with our day yesterday, which made me feel as if the light were reappearing at the end of a long tunnel. . . .
Excuse me if today I return to little questions, essential ones all the same.

I think it's essential to have the photograph from the Musée Guimet, *The Vi-dam and His Sakati*, which is in Malraux's book (the first one published in the NRF series on art).
René Magritte lives at 97, rue des Mimosas, Bruxelles 3. And it is very important to write to get the color version of the *Carnaval de Sage*, either from Magritte himself or from the editor, or from both.

We didn't talk yesterday about the frescoes from the Villa of Mysteries in Pompeii, of which you have the photographs.

Regarding the Dionysic vases, here are some references which should help us get at least some of them.

> 1) in the Louvre, Coupe Cr. no. 160.
> 2) in the Louvre (probably, but maybe at the Bibliothèque Nationale) Amphora from Amasis (Luynes collection)
> 3) Medaillon Cabinet, no. 357.

I think in fact you should find the book by L. B. Lawler pretty easily in the Medaillon Cabinet: *The Maenads* (*Mem of the American Academy in Rome VI*, 1927), in which there is a reproduction of the Munich Amphora 2344 (Lawler, plate XXI, 4). Above all, don't forget about the photograph to be taken from the Museum of Man in the bulletin of prehistoric France, 1954 (or 5), in the article on Venus and Magdalen (the more sensual of the two). This is important; it is the most (by far) clearly erotic of the prehistoric photographs.

Now, an important question: can you make a copy as soon as possible of the last pages of the chapter on prehistory, let's say the last two pages. How can I finish without having these last pages— better say the last three pages. Unless you think it possible that you could get by with an addition to the proofs, which I could easily limit to one or two pages of text.

I have to say, I am very tired, and I'm having a lot of trouble getting back to work. However, your visit to Fontenay was a great comfort to me. . . .

Warmest regards,

G. B.

16

Fontenay, 2 March 1961

My dear friend,

As you see, I'm not yet done bothering you about the illustrations. You will find at Estampes a beautiful—and horrifying—engraving by Cranach, representing a man hung naked by his feet from a horizontal bar, whom an executioner is sawing in two at the crotch. It's important for me from the point of view of the mixture of the erotic and the sadistic, and I don't think it should be hard to find. The title of the engraving is *La Scie* (*The Saw*). *

I received a letter from René Magritte yesterday. He suggests that he take care of asking the Belgian Ministry of Public Education to lend us the necessary photographs for the color reproduction of the *Carnaval du Sage* (naked woman with long blond hair, wearing a mask of a white wolf). I am writing to Magritte to ask him to have the transparencies sent to you at the rue Blomet. I think it would be good if you wrote to him to confirm that this is rather urgent. But Magritte is a little touchy and you should probably not mention the erotic side of things (especially the amusing side of eroticism).[. . .]

I have found, quite by chance—in Fontenay— another photograph of the Chinese torture of the hundred pieces. It's exactly the same torture, but with another man. I have written to our friend Jacques Pimpaneau who would be able, I think, to find the book by a certain Dr.

* See p. 88

Matignon, dating from the beginning of the twentieth century, from which the photograph is taken.

About this torture, I notice that the photographs in my dossier don't include the text that you composed to accompany them.
Could you tell me what's going on with this?
It looks like we don't have anything by Jerome Bosch.[. . .]

G. B.

Orléans, 22 May 1961

My dear friend,

It looks like this might be the last thing I send you. . . . I imagine you will be returning to Paris at the end of the week: at that point we can easily call one another.

I am writing to the Galerie Louise Leiris to try to get the dates of the drawings by Masson; to Pierre Klossowski for the title of the drawing representing a decapitated man, his head between his legs; to Leonor Fini for the title of the painting showing three women one of whom, in the foreground, is in armor. I am giving them your address at the Carlton. If you get to Paris earlier, you have the address and the telephone.[. . .]

As far as the color plates are concerned, I can't really understand things from the page numbers, but I am muddled and very tired. I hope your documents are clearer than mine. If I am going anywhere, which isn't likely, I'll let you know.

The most troublesome thing, and it's really impossible, is the placing of the Capuletti, which you have placed in the middle of the horrors and the tortures, which cannot be interrupted in this way. This absolutely disrupts the logic of these illustrations. It absolutely must be changed. Moreover, it seems to me that the Magritte and the Balthus might also be misplaced. In any case, you must find a way to put the Capuletti before the "Voodoo sacrifice–Chinese torture–final illustrations" sequence; in any event before p. 199. It bothers me to have to demand something so categorically. I do so only, believe me, because I am *obliged to,* absolutely.

In deepest friendship,

G. B.

FOREWORD

We are finally beginning to see the absurdity of any connection between eroticism and morality.

We know that it originated in the connection between eroticism and the most distant superstitions of religion.

But beyond historical exactitude, we shall never lose sight of this principle: either we are obsessed primarily by what desire, by what burning passion suggests to us; or we can with reason hope for a better future.

There is, it seems, a middle course.

I can live in the hope of a better future. But I can still project this future into another world. A world into which I can be introduced only by death.

This middle course was no doubt inevitable. The time came for man to count—more heavily than on anything else—on the rewards, or the punishments that might come about after death.

But finally we begin to see the time when such fears (or such hopes) no longer hold good, and immediate interests will conflict, without a middle course, with future interests—when burning desire will conflict straightaway with the reflective calculations of reason.

No one can imagine a world where burning passion would definitively cease to trouble us. No one, on the other hand, can envisage the possibility of a life that would no longer be bound by calculation.

Civilization in its entirety, *the possibility of human life*, depends upon a reasoned estimation of the means to assure life. But this life—this civilized life—which we are responsible for assuring, cannot be reduced to these *means*, which make it possible. Beyond calculated means, we look for the *end—or the ends*—of these means.

It is banal to devote oneself to an end when that end is clearly only a means. The quest for wealth—sometimes the wealth of egoistic individuals, sometimes wealth held in common—is obviously only a means. Work is only a means.

The response to erotic desire— and to the perhaps most human (least physical) desire of poetry, and of ecstasy (but is it so decisively easy to grasp the difference between eroticism and poetry, and between eroticism and ecstasy?)—the response to erotic desire is, on the contrary, an end.

In fact, the search for means is always, in the last instance, reasonable. Searching after an end arises out of desire, which often defies reason.

In myself, the satisfaction of a desire is often opposed to my interests. But I give in to it, for in a brutal way it has become for me the ultimate end!

It would however be possible to state that eroticism is not only this end that fascinates me. It is not, to the extent that the birth of children can be its consequence. But only *the care* that these children will demand can humanly have a use value. No one would confuse erotic activity—from which the birth of children can result—with this useful work, without which these children would in the end suffer and die.

Utilitarian sexual activity is in conflict with eroticism in that the latter is the ultimate end of our life. But procreation, pursued in a calculated way, like the work of the scythe, risks being reduced in human terms to a lamentable mechanical activity.

The essence of man as given in sexuality—which is his origin and beginning—poses a problem for him that has no other outcome than wild turmoil.

This turmoil is given in the "little death." How can I fully *live* the "little death" if not as a fore-taste of the final death?

The violence of spasmodic joy lies deep in my heart. This violence, at the same time, and I trem-ble as I say it, is the heart of death: it opens itself up in me!

The ambiguity of this human life is really that of mad laughter and of sobbing tears. It comes from the difficulty of harmonizing reason's calculations with these tears. . . . With this horrible laugh. . . .

*

With its first step, this book's meaning is the opening up of consciousness to the identity of this "little death," and of definitive death. From sensuous pleasure, from madness, to a horror without limits.

This is *the first step.*

Which brings us to the forgetting of the puerility of reason!

Of a reason that was never able to measure its limits.

These limits are given in the fact that, inevitably, the *end* of reason, which exceeds reason, is not opposed to the *overcoming* of reason!

In the violence of the overcoming, in the disorder of my laughter and my sobbing, in the excess of raptures that shatter me, I seize on the similarity between a horror and a voluptuousness that goes beyond me, between an ultimate pain and an unbearable joy!

PART ONE

THE BEGINNING

(The Birth of Eros)

In an underground cavern at Laussel, overt sexual union. Bas-relief from the Aurignacian period. Two people lying on their backs opposite one another. One of the figures is a woman. The other, a man, is disappearing under the woman. (The Abbé Breuil accepts this as a rational interpretation.)

Cf. Dr. G. Lalanne: "Découverte d'un bas-relief à représentation humaine dans les fouilles de Laussel," *L'Anthropologie*, vol. XXII, 1911, pp. 257–260.

THE CONSCIOUSNESS OF DEATH

1. EROTICISM, DEATH AND THE 'DEVIL'

The simple sexual act is different from eroticism; the former is found in animal life, whereas human life alone admits of an activity defined perhaps by a "diabolical" aspect, aptly described by the word eroticism.

The word "diabolical," it is true, refers to Christianity. It would appear, however, that even when Christianity was still far off, the most ancient form of humanity knew eroticism. The documents from our prehistory are striking: the first images of man, painted on the walls of caves, show him with his sex erect. There is nothing exactly "diabolical" about these images: they are prehistoric, and the devil in those days, in spite of everything. . . .

If it is true that "diabolical" means essentially the coincidence of death and eroticism, and if the devil is in the end only our own madness, if we come to tears, if we shudder in sorrow—or if we are seized by fits of laughter—can we fail to perceive, linked to this nascent eroticism, the preoccupation with, the haunting fear of death (of a tragic death, in a sense, even though laughable in spite of everything)? These people, who in the images they left of themselves on the walls of caves chose to represent themselves most often with an erection, differed from animals not just on account of the desire thereby associated, in principle, with the essence of their being. What we know about them enables us to say that they knew what animals do not know: that they would die.

I

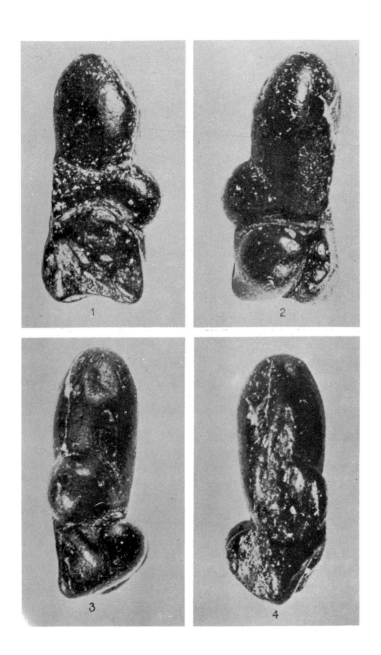

A "sculpted pun" from the Aurignacian (?) period: small figure found near Lake Trasimeno.

Cf. Paolo Graziosi: "Une nouvelle statuette préhistorique," *Bull. de la Société préhistorique française,* vol. XXXVI, 1939, p. 159.

From very ancient times men had a tremulous awareness of death. The images of men with their sex erect date from the Upper Paleolithic. They number among the most ancient of figurations (they precede us by twenty to thirty thousand years). But the most ancient burial chambers, which accompany this anguished awareness of death, greatly predate these images; for early Paleolithic man, death had already such a heavy—and such a clear—meaning that, like us, he arranged a burial place for the corpses of his own kin.

The "diabolical" sphere, which Christianity was ultimately to invest, as we know, with a sense of anguish, is therefore—in its *essence*—contemporaneous with very early man. In the eyes of those who believed in the devil, the "beyond the grave" was diabolical. But the "diabolic" sphere already existed in an embryonic way from the moment men—or at least the ancestors of their species—having recognized that they were going to die, lived in the expectancy, in the anxiety of death.

2. PREHISTORIC MAN AND THE PAINTED CAVES

A peculiar difficulty is born of the fact that the human being did not evolve all at once. These men who were the first to bury their dead kin, and whose bones are to be found in actual tombs, are from a period very much later than the most ancient of human traces. However, these men who were the first to take care of the corpses of their kin were themselves not yet exactly human. The skulls they left still have apelike characteristics: the jaw is protuberant, and very often the arch of the eyebrows is crowned by a bony ridge. These primitive beings, moreover, did not quite have that upright posture

Pubic triangle carved in limestone. Aurignacian.

Cf. D. Peyrony: "La Ferrassie," *Préhistoire*, vol. III, 1934.

Probably another "sculpted pun"
(a female nude in the form of a
phallus). Aurignacian figure from
Sireuil (Dordogne), seen from the
front, and in miniature from
behind.

Cf. H. Breuil and D. Peyrony:
"Statuette féminine aurignacienne
etc," *Rev. anthropologique*, January–
March 1930E. Saccasyn-Della Santa:
*Les figures humaines du Paléolithique
supérieur eurasiatique* (196), Antwerp,
1947.

The famous Lespugne Venus, ivory statue from the Upper Aurignacian period, seen from the front, in profile, and from behind.

Figure of a woman, Brassempouy (female body known as "The Pear"). Late Middle Aurignacian.

Cf. E. Piette: "La station de Brassempouy," *L'Anthropologie,* vol. VI, Plate I, 1895.

which, morally and physically, defines us—and affirms us in our being. Without doubt, they stood upright: but their legs were not perfectly rigid as are ours. It even seems likely that they had, like apes, a hairy exterior, which covered them and protected them from the cold. It is not only from skeletons and burial chambers that we know about what prehistorians designate by the name of Neanderthal man; we have his tools of sculptured stone, which are more advanced than those of his forefathers, who were in general less human. Moreover, Neanderthal man was fairly quickly succeeded by *Homo sapiens,* who is in all respects similar to us. (In spite of his name, *Homo sapiens* actually *knew* little more than the still apelike being that preceded him, but he was physically similar to us).

Prehistorians give the name *Homo faber* (toolmaking man) to Neanderthal man, and to his predecessors. Indeed, the question of "man" comes about with the appearance of tools adapted to a certain usage and shaped toward a given end. The tool is the proof of knowledge, if one allows that knowledge is essentially "knowing how to." The most ancient traces of archaic man—bones accompanied by tools—were found in North Africa (at Ternifine Palikao), and are estimated to be about a million years old. But the time when man became conscious of death, marked by the first tombs, is already of great interest (particularly on the level of eroticism). This date is very considerably later: in principle it would seem to be a hundred thousand years before our time. Finally, the appearance of our fellow creatures, of beings whose skeletons unequivocally establish them as belonging to our species (if one takes into account not the scattered remains of bones but rather the numerous tombs linked to a whole civilization) brings us to no more than thirty thousand years ago.

Thirty thousand years. But by this time we are no longer dealing with human debris recovered through excavations and offered to scientists and prehistorians, who interpret them, necessarily, rather dryly.

We are dealing now with amazing signs, signs that touch our deepest sensibilities: these signs have a force that moves us, and no doubt they will never cease to trouble us. These signs are the paintings that very early man left on the walls of the caves where he must have celebrated his incantatory ceremonies.

Left: Woman, bas-relief from Laussel (Upper Aurignacian).
Right: Statue from Sireuil [profile], (Middle Aurignacian).

Musée de l'Homme, Paris

Another famous statue from the Upper Aurignacian: the Willendorf Venus.

Museum of Natural History, Vienna

Cf. J. Szombatty: *L'Anthropologie*, vol. XXI, 1910, p. 699.

Before the arrival of late Paleolithic man, to whom prehistorians refer by a name scarcely justifiable (*Homo sapiens*),[1] the earliest man seems to have been merely an intermediary between the animals and us. In his very obscurity, this being necessarily fascinates us; but, taken as a whole, the traces he left behind hardly add anything to this undefined fascination. What we know about him, and what touches us most intimately, is not something that pertains primarily to our senses. If we draw from his funeral practices the conclusion that he was conscious of death, we are most immediately moved only at the level of reflection. But Upper Paleolithic man, *Homo sapiens*, is now known to us through signs that move us not only in their exceptional beauty (his paintings are often marvelous). These signs affect us more through the fact that they bring us abundant evidence of his erotic life.

The birth of this extreme emotion, which we designate under the name eroticism and which separates man from animals, is without doubt an essential dimension of what prehistoric research can contribute to knowledge.

1. The adjective *sapiens* means endowed with knowledge. But it is evident that a tool presupposes on the part of the one who makes it a knowledge of its purpose. Indeed this knowledge of the purpose of the tool is the basis for all knowledge. On the other hand, knowledge of death, which is what brings sensibility into play and which is, for this very reason, clearly distinct from pure, discursive knowledge, marks a stage in the development of human knowledge. So knowledge of death, which comes long after the knowledge of tools, nonetheless predates the arrival of what prehistory calls by the name of *Homo sapiens*.

Over: pp. 32 and 33
Nude woman of the Menton Grottos. Upper Aurignacian.

Cf. Salomon Reinach: "Statuette de femme nue," *L'Anthropologie,* vol. IX, 1898, pp. 26–31. Musée de Saint-Germain-en-Laye.

3. EROTICISM LINKED TO THE AWARENESS OF DEATH

The passing of the still somewhat apelike Neanderthal man into our fellow creature, into this fully formed being, whose skeleton in no way differs from our own and whose paintings or engravings, where he is figured, show us that he lost the animal's lush hairy covering, was without doubt decisive. As we have seen, the probably villous Neanderthal man was aware of death. And it is out of this awareness that eroticism appeared, distinguishing the sex life of man from that of the animal. The problem has not been addressed: in principle, the sexual behavior of human beings, which is not, as it is in most animals, seasonal, seems to derive from that of the ape. But the ape is most essentially different from humans in that it is not conscious of death. The behavior of an ape around a dead fellow creature indicates indifference, whereas the still imperfect Neanderthal man, burying the corpses of his kin, does so with a superstitious care that betrays at the same time respect and fear. The sexual behavior of human beings, like that of the ape in general, arises from an intense excitation, uninterrupted by any kind of seasonal rhythm; but it is also characterized by a reserve unknown in animals and which apes in particular never display. In truth, the feeling of embarrassment in regard to sexual activity recalls, in one sense at least, the feeling of embarrassment in regard to death and the dead. "Violence" overwhelms us *strangely* in each case: each time, what happens is *foreign* to the received order of things, to which this violence each time stands in opposition. There is an indecency about death, no doubt distinct from what is incongruous about the sexual act. Death is associated with tears; and sometimes sexual desire is associated with laughter. But laughter is not so much the contrary of tears as it may seem: the object of laughter and the object of tears are always related to some kind of violence which interrupts the regular order of things, the usual course of events. Tears are usually linked to unexpected events that distress us, but on the other hand an unexpected and happy result sometimes moves us to the point of crying. Sexual turbulence obviously does not bring us to tears, but it always disturbs us, sometimes shatters us, and one of two things ensues: either it makes us laugh, or else it impels us to the violence of an embrace.

It is indeed difficult to perceive, clearly and distinctly, how death, or the consciousness of death, forms a unity with eroticism. In its principle, exacerbated desire cannot be opposed to life, which is rather its outcome. The erotic moment is even the zenith of this life, in which the greatest force and the greatest intensity are revealed whenever two beings are attracted to each other, mate, and perpetuate life. It is a question of life, and of reproducing life; but in its reproduction, life overflows, and in overflowing it reaches the most extreme frenzy. These entwined bodies, writhing and swooning, losing themselves in an excess of sensuous pleasure, are in opposition to death, which will later doom them to the silence of corruption.

Indeed, to judge from appearances, eroticism is by all accounts linked to birth, to a reproduction that endlessly repairs the ravages of death.

It is nonetheless true that the animal, the ape, whose sensuality at times becomes exacerbated, knows nothing of eroticism. And this is precisely because it lacks all knowledge of death. To the contrary, it is because we are human and live in the somber perspective of death that we know this exacerbated violence of eroticism.

Speaking from within the utilitarian limits of

Headless woman of Sireuil (Middle Aurignacian).

reason, we can see the practical sense and the necessity of sexual disorder. But for their part, were those who gave the name of "little death"† to the culminating moment wrong to have perceived its funereal sense?

4. DEATH AT THE BOTTOM OF THE "PIT"‡ IN THE LASCAUX CAVE

Is there not in our obscure, *immediate* reaction to death and eroticism, in the way I believe they can be understood, a decisive value, a fundamental value?

I began by speaking of a "diabolical" aspect in the oldest images of man to have come down to us.

But does this "diabolical" element, namely the curse linked to sexual activity, really appear in these images?

I want to introduce the most weighty of questions, with a view to finding in the oldest prehistoric documents a theme illustrated in the Bible. Finding, or at least saying that I have found, in the deepest parts of the Lascaux cave, the theme of original sin, the theme of the Biblical legend! Death linked to sin, linked to sexual exaltation, to eroticism!

In any event, within this cave, in a kind of pit, which is simply a barely accessible natural crevice, there lies a disturbing enigma.

---

†Cf. Bataille, *Erotism: Death and Sensuality,* trans. Mary Dalwood (San Francisco: City Lights, 1986): "Pleasure is so close to ruinous waste that we refer to the moment of climax as a 'little death' (*la petite morte*)," p. 170.

‡*Puits* has sometimes been translated as "well."

In the form of an exceptional painting, the Lascaux man has found a way to inter in the depths this enigma, which he lays before us. To be quite accurate, it was not an enigma from his point of view. For him, the painting of this man and this bison had a clear meaning. But today, we can only despair before the obscure image displayed on the walls of a cave: a man with a bird's face, who asserts his being with an erect penis, but who is falling down. This man is lying in front of a wounded bison. The bison is about to die, but, facing the man, it spills its entrails horrifically.

Something obscure, strange, sets apart this pathetic scene, to which nothing in our time can be compared. Above this fallen man, a bird drawn in a single stroke, on the end of a stick, contrives to distract our thoughts.

Further away, toward the left, a rhinoceros is moving away, but it is surely not linked to the scene where the bison and the man-bird appear, united in the face of death.

As the Abbé Breuil has suggested, the rhinoceros might be moving slowly away from the dying figures after having torn open the stomach of the bison. But clearly the composition of the image attributes the origin of the wound to the man, to the spear that the hand of the dying figure could have thrown. The rhinoceros, on the contrary, seems independent of the principal scene, which, moreover, might remain forever unexplained.

What can one say about this striking evocation, buried for thousands of years in these lost and, so to speak, inaccessible depths?

Inaccessible? Today, for exactly twenty years now, it has been possible to admit a maximum of four people at a time to view this image, which I would oppose to and at the same time link with the

Images of man with erect phallus date from the Upper Paleolithic era. They number among the most ancient of figurations (they precede use by twenty to thirty thousand years). Cf. pp. 11–13.

Ithyphallic figure from the Magdalenian era. Sketched at Altamira.

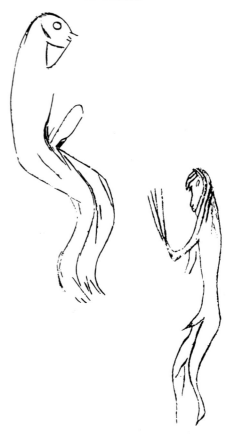

Phallic figure from the grotto at Gourdan, Magdalenian era. Carved on a club with a hole bored through it.

Cf. Piette (ed.): *L'art pendant l'ĝe du renne*, Paris, 1907.

legend of Genesis. The Lascaux cave was discovered in 1940 (on September 12th to be exact). Since then, a small number of people have been able to go down to the bottom of the pit, but the exceptional painting has become quite widely known through photographs. This painting, let me reiterate, represents a man with a bird's head, perhaps dead, but in any case lying in front of a dying bison, which is in the throes of rage.

In a work written six years ago on the Lascaux cave,[2] I forbade myself from giving a personal interpretation of this surprising scene. I restricted myself to relaying the interpretation of a German anthropologist[3] who compared it to a Yakut sacrifice and saw in the posture of the man the ecstasy of a shaman apparently disguised, by means of a mask, as a bird. This shaman—a sorcerer—from the Paleolithic age, would not differ very greatly from a Siberian shaman or sorcerer of modern times. To tell the truth, this interpretation has in my view only one merit: it underlines the "strangeness of the scene."[4] However, after two years of hesitating, it seemed possible, for want of a precise hypothesis, to make an assumption. In a new work,[5] basing myself on the fact "that expiation regularly follows upon the killing of an animal among peoples whose way of life is probably similar to that of the cave artists," I stated:

2. G. Bataille, *Lascaux or the Birth of Art,* trans. Austryn Wainhouse. (Geneva: Skira, 1955).

3. H. Kirchner, "Ein Beitrag zur Urgeschichte der Schamanismus," in Anthropos, vol. 47, 1952.

4. It also underlines the fact that late Paleolithic man was not after all so different from certain Siberian people of modern times. But the details of this comparison seem fragile and hardly tenable.

5. G. Bataille, *Erotism: Death and Sensuality,* trans. Mary Dalwood (San Francisco: City Lights Books, 1986), p. 75.

"The subject of this famous[6] painting, which has called forth numerous contradictory and unsatisfactory explanations, would therefore be *murder and expiation*."

The shaman would be expiating, through his own death, the murder of the bison. Expiation for the murder of animals killed in the hunt is a rule for many tribes of hunters.

Four years having passed, this statement seems to me to be excessively cautious. In the absence of any supporting commentary, such an affirmation had little meaning. In 1957, I again limited myself to saying:

"This view has at least the virtue of replacing the magical (and utilitarian) interpretation of cave pictures, so evidently insufficient, by a religious one more in keeping with the nature of some supreme game. . . .

Today, it seems to me essential to go beyond this. In this book the enigma of Lascaux will not be our sole concern, but at least it will be, in my eyes, the point of departure. And around this enigma I will try to show the meaning of a facet of man it would be futile to neglect or omit, one that is designated by the name of *eroticism*.

6. Famous at least in the sense that so much has been written about it.

Man with a bird's head, detail from
the scene in the pit of the Lascaux
cave. Around 13,500 B.C.

Cf. G. Bataille: *Lascaux, or the Birth
of Art,* trans. Austryn Wainhouse,
Geneva, 1955.

WORK AND PLAY

1. EROTICISM, WORK AND THE 'LITTLE DEATH'

I should first of all take things up from further back. In principle, I could certainly speak about eroticism in detail without having to say too much about the world in which it plays a part. It would however seem futile to speak of eroticism independently of birth, independently of the first conditions under which it came about. Only the *birth* of eroticism, from out of animal sexuality, can bring forth what is essential about it. It would be useless to try to talk about eroticism if we were unable to speak about what it was at its inception.

I cannot fail to evoke in this book the universe of which man is the product, the universe from which he is in fact distracted by eroticism. If, to begin the history of origins, we look at history, the misunderstanding of eroticism has entailed some obvious errors. But if, in wanting to understand man in general, I want in particular to understand eroticism, I am essentially beholden to this initial imperative: from the outset, I must give first place to work. From one end of history to the other, in fact, the first place belongs to work. Work, beyond all doubt, is the foundation of the human being as such.

From one end of history to the other, beginning with the origins (that is to say with prehistory) . . . The field of prehistory, moreover, is no different from history except for the paucity of documents on which it is based. But on this fundamental point, it must be said that the most ancient evidence, and the most abundant, concerns work. Beyond this we

have found some bones, either those of the men themselves or of the animals they hunted—and on which, it seems, they nourished themselves. But among all the documents and evidence that enable us to shed a little light on our most distant past, tools made of stone are by far the most numerous.

The research of prehistorians has furnished innumerable carved stones, which can often be approximately dated according to their location. These stones have been worked so as to fulfill some use. Some served as weapons, and others as tools. The tools, which were used in the making of new tools, were at the same time necessary for the making of weapons: projectiles, axes, and arrow tips, which could be made of stone, but for which the base ma-

Bison with human rear legs and phallus. Caverne des Trois Frères, Sanctuary.

Scene from which the detail (above) is taken. Caverne des Trois Frères.

Cf. Heney Bégouën and H. Breuil: "Les Cavernes du Volp," *Arts et Métiers Graphiques,* Paris, 1958.

terial was sometimes furnished by the bones of dead animals.

Of course, it is work that separated man from his initial animality. It is through work that the animal became human. Work was, above all else, the foundation for knowledge and reason. The making of tools and weapons was the point of departure for that early faculty of reason which humanized the animal we once were. Man, manipulating matter, figured out how to adapt it to whatever end he assigned to it. But this operation changed not only the stone, which was given the desired form by the splinters he chipped from it, but man himself changed. It is obviously work that made of him a human being, the reasonable animal we are.

Mythic scene. Man-bison preceded by an animal which is half stag and half bison, and by a reindeer with palmate front feet.

Cf. "Les Cavernes du Volp," *op. cit.*

But if it is true that work is our origin, if it is true that work is the key to humanity, human beings, through work, ended up distancing themselves completely from animality. And they distanced themselves in particular on the level of their sexual life. At first they adapted their work activity to conform to whatever usefulness it held for them. But it was not through work alone that they developed: in all areas of their life they made their activities and their behavior respond to a given end. The sexual activity of animals is instinctive; the male who seeks out the female and covers her is responding only to an instinctual excitation. But human beings, having achieved through work the consciousness of a sought-after end, came in general to be distanced from the purely instinctual response, in that they discerned the meaning that this response had for them.

For the first humans to become conscious of it, the aim of the sexual act must not have been the birth of children, but rather the immediate pleasure which resulted from it. The instinctual movement

Cavernes des Trois Frères, Sanctuary. The horned god. Close-up view, greatly deformed by the perspective.

Cf. "Les Cavernes du Volp," *op. cit.*

The horned god, relief by H.
Breuil after his tracing.

Cf. "Les Cavernes du Volp," *op. cit.*

Human scene (carved on bone, Isturitz grotto). Early Magdalenian.

Cf. René de Saint-Périer: "Deux oeuvres d'art," *Anthropologie,* vol. XLII, 1932, p. 23, fig. 2.

was shifting in the direction of an association between a man and a woman with the aim of nourishing children, whereas within the limits of animality such an association only took on meaning as the consequence of procreation. Procreation was at the outset not at all a conscious aim. When the moment of sexual union first came to be related to conscious desire by human beings, the end sought was pleasure; it was the intensity, the violence of pleasure. Within the framework of consciousness, sexual activity was at first a response to a calculated seeking after voluptuous pleasures. Even in our times, archaic tribes have remained unaware of any necessary relationship between voluptuous union and the birth of children. For humans, this union of lovers or spouses had at first only one meaning, and that was erotic desire: eroticism differs from the animal sexual impulse in that it is, in principle, just as work is, the conscious searching for an end, for sensual pleasure. This end is not, as it is in work, the desire to acquire something, the desire for increment. Only the child represents an acquisition, but primitive man did not see in this effectively beneficial acquisition of the child the result of sexual union. For civilized man, in general, bringing a child into the world lost the beneficial—materially beneficial—meaning it had for primitive peoples.

Sex for pleasure viewed as an end is no doubt often misprized in our times. It does not conform to the principles on which this activity is founded today. In fact the pursuit of sensual pleasure, although not condemned, is nevertheless viewed in such a way that it is often not open to discussion. To a great extent, moreover, this reaction, which at first sight seems unjustifiable, is nonetheless logical. In a primitive reaction, which never completely ceases to be operative, sensual pleasure is the anticipated result of erotic play. But the result of work is gain: work enriches. If eroticism is viewed in the perspective of desire, independently of the possible birth of a child, it results in a loss, hence the paradoxically valid term "little death." The "little death" has little to do with death, with the cold horror of death. But is the paradox altered when eroticism is in play?

In fact, man, whose consciousness of death distinguishes him from the animal, distances himself further to the extent that in his case eroticism substitutes voluntary play, a calculation of pleasure, for the blind instincts of the organs.

2. DOUBLY MAGICAL CAVES

The burial chambers of Neanderthal man hold this fundamental significance for us: they testify to the consciousness of death, to the awareness of the tragic fact that man can, that he must, founder in death. But we can only be sure of this passage from instinctual sexual activity to eroticism with respect to the period when our fellow creature appeared, this man of the late Paleolithic, the first who was in no way our inferior physically and who was perhaps, and we must indeed assume so, possessed of mental resources similar to our own.[8] There is even

8. In principle, a child of the late Paleolithic era, educated in our schools, could have reached the same level as we have.

nothing to prove that this very early man suffered from the (in fact very superficial) inferiority which we attribute to those we sometimes call "savages" or "primitives." Are not the paintings of his era, which are the first known paintings, comparable at times to the works of art in our museums?

Neanderthal man manifested one more inferiority which distinguished him from us. Without doubt, like us (and like his ancestors) he stood in an upright position. But he still kept his legs a little bent and furthermore he did not walk "like a human;" he stepped on the ground with the edge of his foot and not the sole. He had a low forehead, a protuberant jaw, and his neck was not, like ours, long and slender. It is even logical to imagine him as being covered with hair as are apes and mammals in general.

We really do not know anything about the disappearance of this archaic man, except that our fellow creature occupied unchanged the regions that Neanderthal man had peopled. For example, he flourished in the Valley of Vézère and in other regions (in the southwest of France and the north of Spain) where numerous traces of his admirable talents have been discovered. The birth of art, in fact, followed upon the physical completion of the human being.

It is work that was decisive: it was the virtue of work that determined intelligence. But the ultimate consummation of man, this accomplished human nature, which at first began to enlighten us and ended up endowing us with a feeling of exhilaration, initiated a sense of satisfaction not merely the result of a useful task. At the moment when, hesitantly, the work of art appeared, work had been for hundreds of thousands of years a fact of human life. In the end, it is not work, but *play,* that marked the advent of art and the moment when work became in part, in

Opposite: One of the Venuses discovered in 1952 by Vesperini in La Magdaleine, a hamlet on the shores of the Aveyron. ". . . The most remarkable sculptures of the Magdalenian era" (H. Breuil).

Cf. B. Bétirac: "La Vénus de la Magdaleine," *Bulletin de la Société française préhistorique,* vol. LI, pp. 125–26. Cf. also two plates in R. Vergnes: *Gravures magdaléniennes, etc.* id., vol. XLIX, no. 11–12, pp. 622–24, 1952 (reliefs).

genuine masterpieces, something other than a response to the concern for utility. Indeed, man is essentially an animal who works. But he also knows how to change work into play. I would emphasize this in the context of art (of the birth of art): human play, truly human play, was first of all work, work that became play.[9] What ultimately is the meaning of the marvelous paintings that untidily adorn these almost inaccessible caves? These caves were somber sanctuaries faintly lit by torches; these paintings, it

Two reliefs by two different scholars (Bétirac and Vergnes).

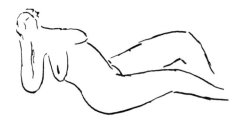

9. I am unable within the limits of this book to make any clearer the primary, decisive character of work.

is true, were supposed to bring about magically the death of the beasts and the birds they represented. But their fascinating animal beauty, forgotten for thousands of years, still has a primal meaning, one of seduction and passion, of wondrous *play,* of breathtaking play, behind which lies the desire for success.

These cave sanctuaries are, essentially, arenas of play. In these caves, pride of place is given to the hunt, by reason of the magical value of the paintings, and perhaps also the beauty of the figurations: the more beautiful they were, the greater their effect. But in the charged atmosphere of these caves it was seduction, the profound seduction of play that was no doubt preeminent, and it is in this sense that there are grounds for interpreting the association of the animal figures of the hunt with the human erotic figures. Such an association is certainly not in any way prejudicial. It would make more sense to invoke chance. But it is certain that these somber caves were actually consecrated above all else to what is, at bottom, play—play as opposed to work, play whose essence is above all to obey seduction, to respond to *passion.* Now passion, introduced, it seems, wherever human figures appeared, painted or drawn on the walls of prehistoric caves, is eroticism. The dead man in the Lascaux pit aside, many of these figures are masculine and have an erect penis. There is even a female figure who is quite obviously expressing desire. Finally, the image at Laussel of a couple sheltered under the rocks openly represents sexual union. The freedom of these early times has something of a paradisiac nature. It is probable that these rudimentary civilizations, which were however most vigorous in their simplicity, knew nothing of war. The civilization of the Eskimos today, who were themselves ignorant of war before the white man arrived, has none of its essential vir-

tues. It does not have the supreme virtue of the dawn of humanity. But the climate of prehistoric Dordogne was similar to that of the arctic regions where the Eskimos live today. And the Eskimos' sense of festivity was no doubt not foreign to those who were our distant ancestors. In response to some ministers who wanted to oppose their sexual freedom, the Eskimos said that up until then they had lived freely and gaily in a manner similar to the birds that sing. The cold, no doubt, is less of a hindrance to erotic games than we, with our present comforts, might imagine. The Eskimos give proof of this. Likewise, on the high plateaus of Tibet, known for a polar climate, the inhabitants are devoted to these games.

There is perhaps a paradisiac aspect to early eroti-

"Erotic statue from the desert of Judea" (found at Mar Khareïstoun). End of Paleolithic era.

Cf. René Neuville: *Anthropologie,* vol. XLIII, 1933, pp. 558–60.

cism, naive traces of which we still find in caves. But this aspect is not clear, for its childlike naiveté was already beset by a certain heaviness.

Tragic . . . And without the slightest doubt.

At the same time, from the outset, comic.

Because eroticism and death are linked.

And because, at the same time, laughter and death, and laughter and eroticism, and linked. . . .

We have already seen eroticism linked to death in the depths of the Lascaux cave.

There is in that place some strange revelation, a fundamental revelation. But such that we surely cannot be surprised by the silence—by the uncomprehending silence which only so meaningful a mystery can harbor.

The image is all the more strange in that this dead figure with his sex erect has a bird's head, an animal's head which is so childish that perhaps, obscurely, tentatively, a laughable aspect emerges.

The proximity of a bison, a dying monster losing its entrails, a kind of minotaur which, it appears, this ithyphallic dead man has killed—there is probably no other image in the world so laden with comic horror; nor, moreover, so unintelligible.

We have here a desperate enigma, laughable in its cruelty, posed at the dawn of time. It is not really a question of solving this enigma. But however true it is that we lack the means to solve it, we cannot just turn away from it; it invites us at least to dwell in its depths.

Being the first enigma posed by humans, it asks us to descend to the bottom of the abyss opened in us by eroticism and death.

No one suspected the origin of animal images would be glimpsed by chance in some subterranean gallery. For millennia, prehistoric caves and their paintings had in some way disappeared: an absolute silence was becoming eternal. Even at the end of the last century, no one would have guessed the astounding ancientness of those paintings that chance had uncovered. It was only at the beginning of the present century that the authority of a great scholar, the Abbé Breuil, confirmed the authenticity of the works of these early men, the first who were truly our fellow creatures but who are separated from us by the immensity of time.

The light has dawned on us today, without there remaining the shadow of a doubt. A ceaseless stream of visitors now animates these caves that have emerged little by little, one after the other, from an infinite night. They are drawn toward one cave in particular, the Lascaux cave, the most beautiful, the richest.

Of all of them, it is this one that remains partially mysterious.

In the deepest crevice of this cave, the deepest and also the most inaccessible (today, however, a vertical iron ladder allows access to a small number of people at a time, so that most of the visitors do not know about it, or at best know it through photographic reproductions), at the bottom of a crevice so awkward to get to that it now goes under the name of the "pit," we find ourselves before the most striking and the most strange of evocations.

A man, dead as far as one can tell, is stretched out, prostrate in front of a heavy, immobile, threatening animal. This animal is a bison, and the threat it poses is all the more grave because it is dying: it is wounded, and under its open belly its entrails are spilling out. Apparently it is this outstretched man who struck down the dying animal with his spear. But the man is not quite a man; his head, a bird's head, ends in a beak. Nothing in this whole image justifies the paradoxical fact that the man's sex is erect.

Because of this, the scene has an erotic character; this is obvious, clearly emphasized, but it is inexplicable.

Thus, in this barely accessible crevice stands revealed—but obscurely—a drama forgotten for so many millennia: it re-emerges, but it does not leave behind its obscurity. It is revealed, but nevertheless it is veiled.

From the very moment it is revealed, it is veiled.

But in these closed depths a paradoxical accord is signed, an accord all the more grave in that it is signed in this inaccessible obscurity. This essential and paradoxical accord is between death and eroticism.

Its truth no doubt continues to assert itself. However, no matter how it asserts itself, it still remains hidden. Such is the nature of both death and eroticism. The one and the other in fact conceal themselves: they conceal themselves at the very moment they reveal themselves.

We cannot imagine a more obscure contradiction nor one better contrived to guarantee disorder in our thinking.

Can we, moreover, imagine a place more conducive to this disorder—the lost depths of this cave, which must never have been inhabited, which must even have been abandoned in the earliest times of human life.[10] (We also know that in the era when our forefathers wandered to this pit in the depths, wanting at all costs to get down into it, they had to lower themselves by the use of ropes.[11])

"The enigma of the pit" is certainly one of the most difficult to bear; at the same time, it is the most tragic one among the enigmas of our species. That it

10. About 15,000 years before our era.

11. A piece of rope has even been found in the cave at Lascaux.

arises from such a very distant past explains the fact that it is posed in terms whose excessive obscurity is at first sight striking. But it is an impenetrable obscurity that has the elementary virtue of an enigma. If we allow this paradoxical principle, then this enigma of the pit (which so strangely and so perfectly corresponds to the fundamental enigma, being the most distant one that a distant humanity poses for humanity today, being the most obscure in its essence), this enigma, then, might also be the one most laden with meaning.

Is it not heavy with that initial mystery, which is in itself the coming into the world, the advent, of man? Does it not at the same time link this mystery to eroticism and death?

The truth is that it is futile to introduce an enigma at once so essential, and yet posed in the most violent form, independently of a well-known context, a context that, however, remains in essence veiled by reason of the very structure of human beings.

It remains veiled to the extent that the human mind hides from itself.

Veiled, in the face of oppositions that vertiginously disclose themselves, in these nearly inaccessible depths which are, for me, "the extremities of the possible."

Such oppositions would be, in particular:

The indignity of the ape, which does not laugh . . .

The dignity of man, who can however "split his sides" laughing . . .

The complicity of the tragic—which is the basis of death—with sensual pleasure and laughter . . .

The intimate opposition between the upright posture—and the anal orifice—linked to squatting . . .

Dionysos and a maenad (detail).
Vase with red figures from the
middle of the fifth century.
See p. 64–65. Louvre no. 421.

PART TWO

THE END

(From Antiquity to the Present Day)

DIONYSOS OR ANTIQUITY

Small shrine of Dionysos (Delos).

I

1. THE BIRTH OF WAR

Very often, the raptures with which we associate the name of Eros have a tragic sense. This aspect is particularly noticeable in the scene in the Lascaux pit. But neither war nor slavery is associated with the earliest times of our own species.

Prior to the end of the late Paleolithic period, war seems to have been unknown. It is only after this time—or after the intermediary period known as the Mesolithic[12]—that we find the first accounts of men killing each other in combat. A rupestrine painting in the Spanish Levant shows an extremely intense battle between archers.[13] This painting, as far as we can tell, dates from about 10,000 years before our era. Let us add only that human societies have continued to devote themselves since then to the practice of war. However, it seems reasonable to believe that in Paleolithic times, murder, by which I mean homicide, was probably not unknown. Still, it was never a question of opposing armed groups trying to annihilate one another. (Even in modern times, homicide occurred, though only exceptionally, among Eskimos who were, like Paleolithic man, unfamiliar with war. Eskimos live in a cold climate comparable in general to the climate of the regions in France where the man of our painted caves lived.)

12. Mesolithic refers to "middle stone," an intermediary between "old stone" (Paleolithic) and "new stone" (Neolithic), or "polished stone."

13. A reproduction of this painting is in my *Erotism,* plate VI.

Monument in the shape of a phallus. Small shrine of Dionysos
(Delos).

In spite of the fact that from its earliest occur-
rence primitive war set one group against another, it
seems likely that it was not at first carried out in any
systematic way. To judge from primitive forms of
war, which are still to be found today, what was at
stake in the beginning was not a material advantage
to be gained.

The victors annihilated the vanquished group. In
the wake of combat they massacred enemy survi-
vors, prisoners, and women. But young children of
both sexes were probably adopted by the victors
who must have granted them the same status as
their own children after the war was over. As far as
we can tell, judging from the practices of modern
primitives, the only material gain from war was the
ultimate growth of the victorious group.

2. SLAVERY AND PROSTITUTION

It was only much later—though we know nothing about the date of this change—that the victors
saw the possibility of putting their prisoners to use
by reducing them to slavery. The possibility of in-
creasing the labor force and decreasing the effort
necessary for the survival of the group was quickly
appreciated. Thus, cattle rearing and agriculture,
which had begun in Neolithic times, prospered because of the increased work force, which in turn allowed for a relative idleness on the part of the
warriors. And complete idleness on the part of their
chiefs.

Before the arrival of war and slavery, embryonic
civilization had been based upon the activity of free
men who were all essentially equal. But slavery was
born of war. Slavery played an important part in the

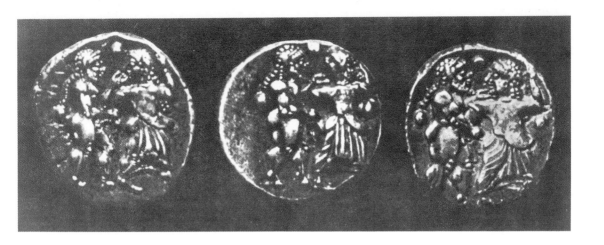

Maenads with ithyphallic characters (Macedonian coins, fifth century B.C.).

Bibliothèque Nationale, Medalion Cabinet. Cf. Jean Babelon: "Un Eldorado macédonien," *Documents,* 2 May, 1929.

division of society into opposing classes. The warriors were able to amass great wealth through war and slavery, simply by endangering, first of all, their own lives, and then by endangering the lives of their fellow men. The birth of eroticism preceded the division of humanity into free men and slaves. But in part, erotic pleasure depended upon social status and the possession of wealth.

In primitive conditions, erotic pleasure was consequent upon the charm, physical vigor, and intelligence of the men, and the beauty and youth of the women. For the women, beauty and youth remained decisive. But this society, which came of war and slavery, believed in the importance of privilege.

The system of privilege made prostitution the normal channel for eroticism, making it dependent on an individual's power or wealth, and dooming it to live as a lie. We should not be mistaken about this: between prehistory and classical antiquity, sexual life went astray, it became ankylose because of war and slavery. Marriage guaranteed a place for

necessary procreation. This place was rendered all the more difficult in that from the beginning the freedom enjoyed by males tended to let them stray from the house. Today, even now, humanity has hardly got out of this rut.

3. THE PRIMACY OF WORK

In the long run, one essential fact is clear: emerging from the misery of the Paleolithic period, humanity encountered evils that must have been unknown in the earliest times. The practice of war apparently dates from the beginning of these new times.[14] Although nothing very precise is known on this subject, the arrival of war on the scene, at least in principle, must have marked the decline of material civilization. The animal art of the late Paleolithic—which lasted some twenty thousand years—disappeared. At least it disappeared from the Franco-Cantabrian region:[15] nowhere did anything as beautiful, as grand, take its place. At least nothing known to us.

Human life, emerging from its initial simplicity, chose the accursed path of war. Ruinous war, war that led to degradation, war that led to slavery, and led in addition to prostitution.[16]

Ithyphallic characters and maenads (Macedonia).

14. Toward the end of the Paleolithic and probably during the transition from the Paleolithic to the Neolithic period, known as the Mesolithic period. See above, p. 57, note 12.

15. Roughly the southwest of France and the north of Spain. See above, p. 46

16. If prostitution was not at first necessarily something degrading (consider for example religious prostitution, sacred prostitution), it very quickly ended up, with the onset of servile poverty, in *base prostitution.*

In the early years of the nineteenth century, Hegel tried to show that the repercussions of war, which stemmed from slavery, also had a beneficial aspect.[17] According to Hegel, contemporary man had little in common with the aristocratic warrior of early times. In principle, contemporary man was the worker. The rich themselves worked, as did in general the dominant classes. They worked, at least in moderation.

It was the slave, in any case, and not the warrior, who by means of work changed the world; and it is the slave, in the end, who is changed in his essence by work. Work changed him to the extent that he became the only authentic creator of the wealth of civilization; in particular, intelligence and knowledge are the fruits of the labor to which the slave was constrained, working in the first place in response to the orders of his master. It is in this way, we should point out, that work engendered man. Those who do not work, who are dominated by the shame of work—the rich aristocrat of the ancien régime or those with private means today—are mere relics. Industrial wealth, which is the pleasure of today's world, is the result of thousands of years' work on the part of the enslaved masses, the unhappy multitude, which since Neolithic times has been composed of slaves and workers.

Henceforth, work is what is decisive in the world. War itself poses above all industrial problems, problems that industry alone can settle.

But, before the idle ruling class, which drew its strength from wars, fell into its present state of degeneration, its idleness tended to detract somewhat from its importance. (Those who leave to others the tedious, exacting effort of work are ultimately beset

Detail from a sixth century amphora, Corinth.

Musée Royal, Brussels. Cf. Ernst Buschor, *Satyränze*, pp. 37–38.

17. In *The Phenomenology of Mind* (1806).

by a veritable curse.) Everywhere, aristocracy fairly quickly gave itself over of its own accord to decadence. This is a principle that was formulated by a Tunisian Arab writer of the fourteenth century. According to Ibn Khaldoun, the victors, who had adopted an urban lifestyle, were one day conquered by nomads, whose tougher life had kept them up to the challenges of war. But we must apply this law to a larger domain. As a general rule, the use of wealth in the long run leads to a greater resilience on the part of the poor. At first, the richest have superior material resources. The Romans maintained their domination because for a long time they had had the advantage of superior military tactics. But a day came when this advantage weakened, because of an increased aptitude for war among the barbarians and also, on the Roman side, a decrease in the number of soldiers.

Satyrs and maenad (detail from a sixth century Greek vase).

Nationalmuseet, Copenhagen.

But the role of military service in wars was significant only in the beginning. Within the limits of a given material civilization, stabilized by a lasting advantage, the underprivileged classes benefit from a moral vigor which, in spite of their material strengths, is lacking in the privileged classes.

We must now turn to the problem of eroticism, whose importance is no doubt secondary, but which has an important place in antiquity, a place it has lost today.

Detail of a Hydra. Epictetos, sixth century.

Louvre

Cf. A. Furtwaengler and Reichhold: *Greichische Vasenmalerei,* plate 73 and Lillian B. Lawler: "The Maenads," *Memoirs of the American Academy,* VI, Rome, 1927.

4. ON THE ROLE OF THE LOWER CLASSES IN THE DEVELOPMENT OF RELIGIOUS EROTICISM

Inasmuch as eroticism had any meaning in antiquity, inasmuch as it had any role in human activity, it was not always to the aristocrats—which meant, in those days, anyone who had attained the privileges of wealth[18]—that this role accrued. Indeed it was above all the religious restlessness of the have-nots in the aristocrats' shadow that determined the meaning of eroticism.

Wealth, of course, played its part. As far as established practices were concerned, marriage and prostitution meant that the possession of women tended to depend on money. But within this brief survey of eroticism in antiquity, I must first of all consider religious eroticism, especially the orgiastic religion of Dionysos. Within the Dionysiac cult, money in principle played no part, or played only a secondary role (like a sickness in the body). Those who took part in Dionysiac orgies were often have-nots, sometimes even slaves. According to the time and the place, social class and wealth varied. (We have hardly any information about this. But we never really have any definite evidence.)

It is impossible to say anything with exactitude about the importance of such a dissolute activity, which seems to have had no uniformity whatsoever. As there was not really any unified Dionysiac church, the rites varied with time and place. Thus we have only a very uncertain knowledge about them.

18. In Greece, at least, a birth that was not backed up by wealth had no legal status.

Nobody took the trouble to inform posterity. No one would have been able to do so with a desired precision.

We can just about say with certainty that before the first centuries of the Roman Empire, at least, aristocratic revelers played no important part in the sects.

In the beginning, in Greece, as far as we can tell, the practice of the Bacchanalia had on the contrary the sense of a surpassing of sensualist eroticism. Dionysiac practices were at first violently religious; it was an enflamed movement, it was a movement of self loss. Yet this movement, on the whole, is so poorly known that the links between the Greek theater and the cult of Dionysos are difficult to locate.

Dancing maenads. Plate signed by the potter Macron and the painter Hieron (400–480 B.C.).

Staatliche Museen, Berlin.

Cf. E. Pfuhl: *Meisterwerke Griechischer Zichnung und Malerei,* 1924, plate 41, fig. 58. E. Buschor: "Satyrtänze und Frühes Drama," *Bayerichen Akademie der Wissenschaften,* Munich, 1943, 3. *Id. Griechenvasen,* plate 155, Munich, 1940.

But it would not be surprising if the origin of tragedy is in some way linked to this violent cult. The
cult of Dionysos was in essence tragic. At the same
time it was erotic, it was so in its frenzied disorder,
but we know that to the extent that the cult of
Dionysos was erotic, it was tragic. Tragic, moreover, above all, and eroticism ended up bringing it
into a domain of tragic horror.

5. FROM EROTIC LAUGHTER
TO PROHIBITION

In considering eroticism, the human mind is
faced with its most fundamental difficulty.

Eroticism, in a sense, is laughable. . . .

Allusion to the erotic is always capable of arous-
ing irony.

Even in speaking of the *tears* of Eros, I could give
in to laughter. . . . Eros is nonetheless tragic. Above
all, Eros is the tragic god.

We know that for the ancients, Eros had a puerile
aspect: it had the face of a young child.

But after all, is not love all the more anguishing
in that it moves us to laughter?

The foundation of eroticism is the sexual act.
Now, this act is subject to a prohibition. It's inconceivable! making love is *prohibited*! Unless you do it
in secret.

But if we do it in secret the prohibition transfig-
ures what it prohibits and illumines it with a glow,
at once sinister[19] and divine: in a word, it illumines
it with a religious glow.

The prohibition gives its own value to what it
prohibits. Often, at the very moment I seize upon

19. The lighting of obscenity, like that of crime, is lugubrious.

A maenad and a silenus. Inside of a plate signed by Hieron.

Cf. Langlotz: *Griechische Vasenbilder*, p. 29, fig. 42, and Lillian B. Lawler: *The Maenads, op. cit.*

Museum antiker Kleinkunst, Munich

Maenad and silenus. Plate.

Louvre (G. 488).

the intention to refrain, I ask myself if, on the contrary, I have not been deceitfully provoked!

Prohibition gives to what it proscribes a meaning that in itself the prohibited action never had. A prohibited act invites transgression, without which the act would not have the wicked glow which is so seductive. In the transgression of the prohibition a spell is cast.

It is not only eroticism that emits this glow. It is a glowing that also illumines religious life each time full violence comes into action, the kind of violence that comes into play when death opens the throat—and ends the life—of the victim.

Satyrs and maenad, fifth century B.C. Detail from a Greek vase.

Fine Arts Museum, Boston. Cf. Ernst Pfuhl: *Meisterwerke etc. op. cit.*

Satyr and maenad. Plate signed by Hieron.

Louvre (G. 144).

Sacred!

In advance, the syllables of this word are burdened with anguish, and the weight which burdens is that of death in the sacrifice. . . .

Our entire life is burdened with death. . . .

But, in me, definitive death has the sense of a strange victory. It bathes me with its glow, it opens in me an infinitely joyous laughter: that of disappearance!

....
....

If I had not, in these few phrases, enclosed myself in that moment when death destroys being, how could I speak about this "little death" in which, without actually dying, I collapse in a feeling of triumph!

6. TRAGIC EROTICISM

There is much more in eroticism than we are at first led to believe.

Today, nobody recognizes that eroticism is an insane world whose depths, far beyond its ethereal forms, are infernal.

I have given a lyrical form to the insight I am now proposing, which would affirm a link between death and eroticism. But on this I insist: unless it is given to us in all its sudden depth, the meaning of eroticism will escape us. Eroticism is first of all the most moving of realities; but it is nonetheless, at the same time, the most ignoble. Even after psychoanalysis, the contradictory aspects of eroticism appear in some way innumerable; their profundity is religious—it is horrible, it is tragic, it is still inadmissible. Probably all the more so because it is divine.

In relation to the simplified reality that is a limit for mankind as a whole, eroticism is a ghastly maze where the lost ones must tremble. This is the only way to come close to the truth of eroticism: to tremble.[20]

Prehistoric man knew this when he linked his excitement to an image buried in the pit of the Lascaux grotto.[21]

The votaries of Dionysos, who were able to conjoin their impulse to that of the bacchantes, were aware of this when, lacking children of their own, they tore with their teeth and devoured live goats.[22]

20. See above, p. 25, and below, p. 142.

21. See above, pp. 34–38.

22. I may seem difficult to understand here; but rather than going on, I refer the reader to the relevant chapters of my book.

7. THE GOD OF TRANSGRESSION AND OF THE FEAST: DIONYSOS

At this point, I would like to explain the religious meaning of eroticism.

The meaning of eroticism escapes anyone who cannot see its *religious* meaning!

Reciprocally, the meaning of religion in its totality escapes anyone who disregards the link it has with eroticism.

First I will try to give an image of religion that in my view[23] accords with its essence, with its origin.

The essence of religion is to single out certain acts as guilty acts, namely prohibited ones.

Religious prohibition proscribes on principle a specific act, but it can at the same time give a value to what it proscribes. It is sometimes even possible, or even prescribed, to violate the prohibition, to transgress it. But above all, the prohibition determines the value—a dangerous value in principle—of that which it denies: roughly, this value is that of the "forbidden fruit" of the first chapter of Genesis.

---

23. It is only in light of this statement of principle about the meaning of religion that a general account of Dionysiac religion can take on meaning.

It is banal to understand religion in terms of morality, which in general makes the value of an act depend upon its consequences. But in religion, acts have essentially their immediate value, a sacred value. It is of course possible (and important) to take a sacred value as something useful (in which case one treats this value as a strength). But a sacred value remains nonetheless in its very principle an immediate value: it has meaning only in the instant of this transfiguration, wherein we pass precisely from use value to ultimate value, a value independent from any effect beyond the instant itself, and which is fundamentally an aesthetic value.

Kant saw where this problem was located, but there is probably an escape built into his statement (if he did not see that his position presupposes, in any judgment, a prior agreement on utility, against utility).

This value turns up again in the feasts, during the course of which what was ordinarily excluded was allowed and even required. Transgression, for the time of the feast, is precisely what gives the feast its marvelous aspect, its divine aspect. Among the gods, Dionysos is the one essentially linked to the feast. Dionysos is the god of the feast, the god of religious transgression. Dionysos is seen most often as the god of the vine and of drunkenness. Dionysos is a drunken god, the god whose divine essence is madness. But, to begin with, madness is itself of divine essence. Divine, which is to say, it denies the law of reason.

We usually associate religion with law and reason. But if we confine ourselves to what grounds religions *as a whole,* we are forced to reject this notion.

Maenad (detail from an amphora attributed to Cleophrades), 500 B.C.

Munich, Museum antiker Kleinkunst. Cf. Pfuhl, *Meisterwerke etc, op. cit.*

Maenad in a trance. Amphora from the fifth century.

Munich (2344).

Maenads and ithyphallic characters (fifth century).

Etruscan vase (fifth or sixth
century B.C.) (copy).

Religion is doubtlessly, even in essence, subversive: it turns away from the observance of laws. At least, what it demands is excess, sacrifice, and the feast, which culminates in ecstasy.[24]

8. THE DIONYSIAC WORLD

In wanting to give a striking image of religious eroticism, I was led to considerations of great complexity. The question concerning the relationships between eroticism and religion is all the more unwieldy in that the religions flourishing today are generally content to deny or exclude them altogether. It is trite to allege that religion condemns eroti-

24. I shall have to give a rather rapid account of the facts in their entirety.

The Triumph of Priapus, post-Renaissance interpretation by Francesco Salviati (1510–1563).

cism, while eroticism is, essentially and in its origins, associated with religious life. The individualized eroticism of our modern civilizations, by reason indeed of this individualistic character, no longer has any link to religion—unless it is in the ultimate condemnation of eroticism's disorder as something opposed to the meaning of religion.[25]

This condemnation, however, is inscribed within the history of religions: its place is a negative one, but it has a place. I say this here parenthetically, being obliged to set aside for another work (inevitably philosophical in nature), the development that such

Roman mosaic, Timgad.

25. One still finds some vague remnants that lend to Christianity (or at least to this opposite of Christianity: Satanism) an erotic aspect; but after Huysmans, Satanism lost the topical value that this writer described at the end of the nineteenth century in *Là Bas.* As far as I can tell, these remnants are nothing more than commercially organized comedies.

Fauns and Bacchant (after a water color, for Hancarville).

an affirmation would require. Indeed, I have arrived at the decisive moment in human life. In casting eroticism out of religion, men reduced religion to a utilitarian morality. Eroticism, having lost its sacred character, became unclean.

I will restrict myself for the moment to moving from these general considerations regarding the cult of Dionysos to a rapid exposition of what we know about certain fairly longstanding practices[26] that brought religious eroticism to the stage most worthy of our attention.

Without any doubt, what we are dealing with here, in its essence, is the persistence of an obsession, which grew out of a purely mythological or ritual existence. Dionysos was the god of transgression and of the feast. He was at the same time, as I have said, the god of ecstasy and madness. Drunkenness, the orgy, and eroticism are the manifest aspects of a god whose traits are blurred in his profound frenzy. Beyond this drunken figure, it is true, we can discern an archaic agricultural divinity. In his oldest form, this figure is related to material and agrarian preoccupations, and is linked to peasant life. But very quickly the concerns of the worker in the fields are left behind for the disorderliness of *drunkenness* and *madness*. In the beginning, Dionysos was not a god of wine. In sixth-century Greece, the cultivation of the vine did not have the importance it was soon to take on.

Dionysiac madness was in fact a restrained madness, considerate of the interests of its victims: only rarely was death the outcome. The frenzy of the

26. A matter of at least a millennium. It seems likely moreover that the Dionysianism of the sixth century was a continuation of some already very ancient customs. It is also possible that the Satanism to which I made reference is linked in general to the continuance of the cult of Dionysos (see pp. 70–72).

The salon at the Villa of Mysteries in Pompeii. Dionysiac scenes. First century A.D.

". . . the beautiful paintings in the Villa of Mysteries in Pompeii allow us to imagine the grandeur attained by refined ceremonies in the first century of our era . . ." Cf. p. 75.

maenads reached such a pitch that only tearing apart living children, their own children, seems to have appeased their fury. We cannot affirm with certainty that such excesses really took place during the rituals. But when they had no children of their own, the frenzied maenads would tear apart and devour young goats—kids whose agonized crying differed little from the weeping of babies.[27]

But if we know about the fury of the Bacchanalia, we know nothing exact about how it developed. Other elements must have been added to it. Images found on Thracian coins help us imagine the derangement that must have reigned during a descent into orgy. These coins represent only the archaic aspects of the Bacchanalia. The images portrayed on vases in the centuries that followed help us see what these rituals were like, where licentiousness was the rule. These late representations, on the other hand, also help us realize that a development took place, after which the inhuman violence of its origins disappeared. The beautiful paintings in the Villa of Mysteries in Pompeii let us imagine the grandeur attained by refined ceremonies in the first century of our era. What we know of the bloody repression of

27. As a child, I was filled with anguish when I used to hear the cries of the young goats in front of my house, as they came under the butcher's knife.

LE TRIOMPHE DE PRIAPE
PORTÉ SUR UN CHAR.
Gravé fur une Pierre de Cornaline

Hancarville.

186 A.D., as recounted by Livy, is the basis of certain doubtful accusations which served as the starting point for a political campaign destined to thwart a debilitating exotic influence. (In Italy, the cult of Dionysos—in spite of there being a Latin Dionysos, the god Liber—was considered an oriental import.) The allegations of Tacitus and the narratives of Petronius lead us to believe that, at least in part, Dionysiac practices degenerated into vulgar debauchery.

On the one hand, we believe that the popularity of Dionysos in the first centuries of the empire was such that his cult might have been considered a serious rival to Christianity. On the other hand, the later existence of a more sober Dionysianism, a decent Dionysianism, seems to indicate that the fear of derangement forced those faithful to Dionysos to renounce the virulence of earlier times.

Pan. Greek vase, fifth century.

London.

Spranger: *Last Judgment* (detail).

Turin.

Like Thierry Bouts and Van der Weyden, Bartholomeus Spranger, although a mannerist, also exploited the "last judgment" in order to represent nudity. Cf. pp 81–82.

THE CHRISTIAN ERA

1. FROM CHRISTIAN CONDEMNATION TO MORBID EXALTATION (OR FROM CHRISTIANITY TO SATANISM)

In the history of eroticism, the Christian religion had this role: to condemn it. To the extent that Christianity ruled the world, it attempted to liberate it from eroticism.

But if we want to come to a conclusion about the consequences of this, we are obviously in a predicament.

Christianity was, in a sense, favorable to the world of work. It valorized work at the expense of sensual pleasure. Of course, it turned paradise into the world of immediate—as well as eternal—satisfaction. But first it made paradise the outcome of an effort, the outcome of labor.

In a sense, Christianity is a link that made the outcome of labor—the labor, primarily, of the ancient world—the prelude of a world of work.

We have increasingly seen how, for the ancient world, the ultimate object of religion was the life beyond the grave, so that supreme value was granted to this final outcome, and then was immediately withdrawn. But Christianity stressed this. To the pleasures of the moment it left only a sense of guilt in relation to the final objective. From the Christian perspective, eroticism compromised or at least delayed the final outcome, paradise.

II

But this tendency had its counterpart: it was through condemnation that Christianity itself attained its burning value.

So it was with Satanism. Satanism, being the negation of Christianity, had meaning only to the extent that Christianity appeared to be true. (However, the negation of Christianity finally came to be the quest for oblivion.)

Satanism had a role—especially toward the end of the Middle Ages—but because of its origin it was deprived of any viability. Eroticism was necessarily linked to this drama. Satanism fatally doomed its followers to the same misfortune that befell it, to that same curse of which Satan was the first victim. Certainly, the possibility of error played a part: the demon, it seems, had the power to bestow good fortune. But such an appearance proved in the end to be deceptive. The inquisition had the power to disabuse.

Fortune, without which eroticism inevitably resulted in *misfortune,* its opposite, could only be sought in ruse and strategy. But as strategy, eroticism lost its grandeur: it was reduced to trickery. In the long run, the trickery of eroticism came to seem its essence. Dionysiac eroticism was an affirmation—like all eroticism, which is in part sadistic—but in this relative trickery, affirmation became more and more oblique.[28]

28. But there was one capital exception: Sade. I will come back to this (pp. 103–128).

Thierry Bouts (1400–1475): *Hell*
(detail)

Louvre.

If the Middle Ages represented nudity,
it was only to show the horror of it. The
female nudes of the Flemish painter
Thierry Bouts do not repel the specta-
tor, but they incarnate the horror of
damnation. In Venice another painter
represented nudity: this was to show the
corpses of victims of the dragon St.
George was to slay. Van der Weyden
brought to the horror of the Last Judgment the nudity Theirry Bouts had
situated in hell (see over). And so, later,
did Spranger. Cf. p. 78.

Carpaccio: *Saint George and the Dragon* (detail)

Venice, S. Giorgio.

2. THE REAPPEARANCE OF EROTICISM IN PAINTING

The Middle Ages assigned a place to eroticism in painting: it relegated it to hell![29] The painters of this time worked for the Church. And for the Church, eroticism was sin. The only way it could figure in painting was as something condemned. Only representations of hell—only repulsive images of sin—could furnish it a place.

Things changed with the Renaissance. They changed, especially in Germany, even before the medieval form was abandoned—from the moment art lovers began buying erotic paintings. Only the richest in those times had the means to commission profane paintings. Engravings were somewhat less expensive. But even engravings were not within everyone's means.

These limits must be taken into account. The reflection of passion depicted in these paintings is dis-

Van der Weyden: *The Last Judgment* (detail)

Hospice de Beaume.

29. See the representation of hell in painting, pages 78, 81, and 82. But in Dante's poem, Paolo and Francesca achieved *sublime* love in hell.

torted. These paintings and engravings do not appeal, as did medieval imagery, to a general audience, a popular forum. But the people themselves were subject to the violence of passion: violence could play a part in the rarefied world from which emerged this art born of the night.

We must indeed take these limits into account. In part, the reflection of passion in these paintings—or in these engravings—is distorted. These paintings and engravings do not translate a common sentiment, as the imagery of the Middle Ages had done. Nonetheless the violence of passion played a part in this erotic art born from the night of the religious world, of this surviving world, which piously cursed all works of the flesh.

The works of Albrecht Dürer, Lucas Cranach, and Baldung Grien appeal to this still uncertain light of day. Because of this, their erotic value is in some way poignant. It did not enter a world ready to welcome it. Here we find a flickering, and even feverish glow. Clearly, the large hats of Cranach's female nudes partake of an obsession to provoke. Today, such is our frivolity that we could be tempted to laugh at them. But we owe more than a feeling of amusement to the man who represented a long saw cutting into the crotch of a naked torture victim, hung by his feet. . . .

From the time that a distant, often brutal eroticism entered into this world, we have found ourselves facing the terrible alliance between eroticism and sadism.

Eroticism and sadism are no less linked in the works of Albrecht Dürer than in Cranach or Baldung Grien. But it is to death—to the vision of death as all-powerful, a terrifying death which nonetheless draws us toward an enchantment laden with all the terrors of witchcraft—it is to death, to

Dürer: *Lucretius*

Hanfstaengl, Munich.

Dürer: *The Death of Orpheus,*
after a painting by Mantegna
(lost).

Kunsthalle, Hamburg.

Dürer: *Couple* (1523).

Cranach: *Death of Lucretius,* one of the five painted by Cranach.

Musée de Besançon.

Cranach: *Venus and Love.*

Galleria Borghese, Rome.

the rot of death, and not to pain, that Baldung Grien links the attraction of eroticism. A little later these associations will disappear: *mannerism* will liberate painting from them! But it is not until the eighteenth century that an eroticism that is sure of itself comes to light: libertine eroticism.

3. MANNERISM

Of all erotic painting, the most seductive to me is that which has been named mannerism. Mannerism is moreover little known today. In Italy, mannerism

"... we owe more than a feeling of amusement to the man who represented a long saw cutting into the crotch of a naked torture victim hung by his feet." Cf. p. 83.

Cranach: *The Saw.*

Bibliothèque Nationale.

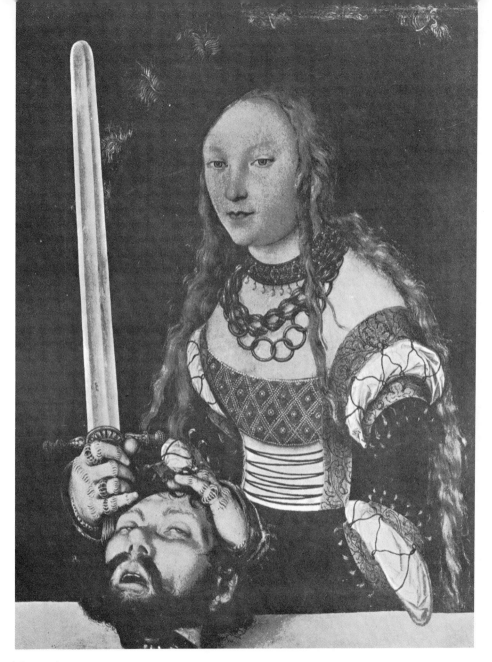

Cranach: *Judith and the Head of Holofernes.*

Gemaeldegalerie, Vienna.

"their erotic value is in some way poignant. It did not enter a world ready to welcome it. Here we find a flickering, even feverish glow." Cf. p. 83.

Hans Baldung Grien: *Love and Death (Vanitas)*, 1510.

Vienna.

Hans Baldung Grien: *Death
and the Woman*, (1515).

Berlin.

Hans Baldung Grien: *The Woman and the Philosopher,* (1513). (Cf. p. 117.)

Hans Baldung Grien: *Judith,* (1515).

Nuremburg.

Hans Baldung Grien: *Lucretius,* (1520).

Frankfurt.

began with Michelangelo. In France, the Ecole de Fontainebleau represented it marvelously. With the exception of Michelangelo,[30] the painters of the

Hans Baldung Grien: *Hercules and Omphale.*

Coll. J. Masson, Ecole des Beaux-Arts, Paris.

30. With the exception of Michelangelo *and* El Greco. But I am speaking only of erotic mannerism here, and as it seems to me, eroticism touches the very essence of mannerism. I should therefore state to what extent and in what way El Greco is related to mannerism. He is related to it in the same way the mysticism of a Saint Angela of Foligno or a Saint Theresa of Avila is linked to a failing Christianity, in which concern over the future—which is essentially what grounds Christianity—has given way to a concern with the present moment (which I said calls for violence, for the intensity of eroticism).

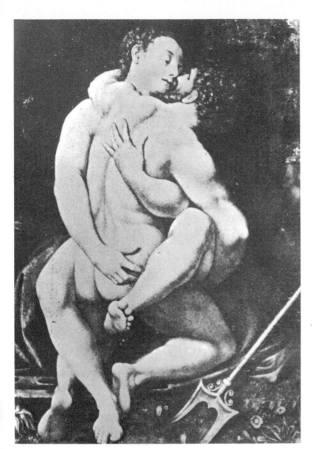

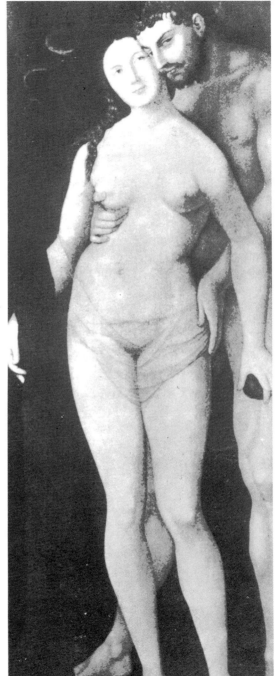

Bernard van Orley (1491–1542):
Neptune and the Nymph.

Brussels.

Hans Baldung Grien: *Adam and Eve.*

Lugano.

mannerist school are little appreciated. They have on the whole gone unrecognized. The Ecole de Fontainebleau ought to have another place in painting. And the names of Caron,[31] Spranger and Van Haarlem do not deserve the oblivion into which they have more or less fallen. They loved the "angel of the bizarre," they revived the forces of sensation. Classicism disdained them. But what is sobriety if not the fear of everything that is not lasting, at least of that which seems as if it will not last. For these same reasons, El Greco himself stopped attracting attention. Most mannerists, it is true, had none of the violence of El Greco—but eroticism harmed them.

31. Antoine Caron (born in Beauvais, 1520; died in Paris, 1598) was trained in the Ecole de Fontainebleau under the direction of the Primatice. His painting is linked to the style of Niccolò dell'Abate, but his "madness" greatly exceeds the scale of his masters and those who inspired him.

Giulio Romano (1492–1562): *Jupiter* (as a dragon) *visits Olympia*.

Fresco, Pavia.

Jan Gossaert: *Metamorphosis of Salmacis into a Hermaphrodite.*

Museum Boymans, Rotterdam.

Flora and Ram. Tapestry after
Bronzino (1502–1572).

Pitti, Florence.

Corregio (1489– 1534): *Jupiter and Io.* Engraving by Francesco Bartolozzi.

Bibliothèque Nationale.

Pontormo [1494–1557] (after Michelangelo): *Leda*.

National Gallery, London.

I should point out that other painters, less bold if no less obsessed, were emerging around the same period, and along similar lines. Tintoretto was El Greco's master, just as Titian was for all practical purposes the master of Tintoretto. But in part because in Italy (particularly in Venice) classicism and its collapse were less felt, the mannerism and the eroticism of Titian—and of Tintoretto—were less disturbing. Whereas El Greco's mannerism so shocked seventeenth-century Spain that the eclipse of one of Europe's most unusual painters lasted very nearly three centuries. In France, where the excesses of El Greco would never have aroused any interest, Poussin's erotic obsession, which at least in principle ran counter to his classicism, apparently encountered no resistance. If he ever betrayed himself, it was above all in an unused sketch (see p. 121).

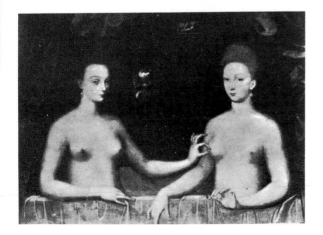

School of Fontainebleau: *Gabrielle d'Estrée and Her Sister.*

Louvre.

School of Fontainebleau:
The Tears of Eros. This painting, long attributed to
Rosso, is known under the
title of "Venus Weeping for
the Death of Adonis."

Musée d'Algers.

4. LIBERTINAGE IN THE EIGHTEENTH CENTURY AND THE MARQUIS DE SADE

A radical change took place in eighteenth-century libertine France. The eroticism of the sixteenth century had been heavy. It could go hand in hand with a frenzied sadism, as it did for example in the work of Antoine Caron. Eroticism in Boucher shifted in the direction of lightness. Lightness might have made an appearance then only to open the way for heaviness. . . . Sometimes laughter sets the stage

School of Fontainebleau: *Diana's Bath* (1545). One of the versions of this painting by François Clouet.

Musée de Tours.

School of Fontainebleau: *Sabina Poppaea.*

Geneva.

School of Fontainebleau: *Woman with Red Lily.*

Coll. of the Marquis de Biencourt, Paris.

for a hecatomb. But the eroticism of those times knew nothing of the horrors to which it was just the prelude.

Boucher probably never met Sade. Whatever excesses of horror may have obsessed him throughout his whole life—and which make up the fierce tales of his books—Sade knew how to laugh.[32] We know, however, that during a brief stopover on the

32. *Philosophy in the Bedroom* is an amusing book: it links horror to amusement.

School of Fontainebleau: *Procris and Cephalis.*

Coll. Seligmann, Musée de l'Orangerie.

School of Fontainebleau: *Mars and Venus.*

Petit Palais.

Kunsthistorisches Museum, Vienna.

Bartholome Spranger: *The Triumph of Wisdom.*

Daniele Ricciardelli (of Volterra): *Saint John the Baptist.*

Galleria Royale, Turin.

The "executioner": detail from the painting by Ricciardelli (1509– 1566).

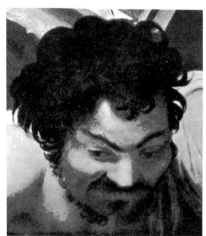

Bartholome Spranger: *Mary Magdalen.*

Bibliothèque Nationale.

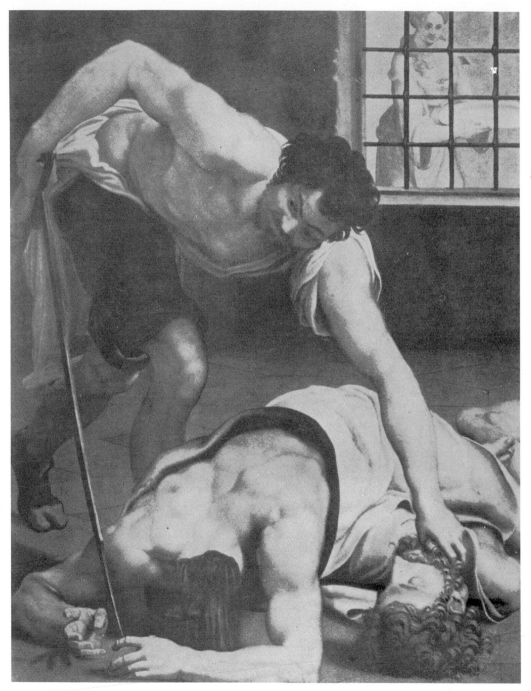

Jacopo   Zucchi   (1541–1589): *Psyche Surprises Love.*

way from the prison at Madelonnettes to one at Pic-
pus, a journey which, had it not been for the Ther-
midorian Reaction, would have ended on the
scaffold, Sade was completely drained by the sight
of those being executed before his very eyes, on the
orders of the Revolution.[33] But the life of Sade himself! He spent thirty years of his life in prison, but,
more than that, he peopled his solitude with innumerable dreams: dreams of terrible screams and
bloodied bodies. Sade endured this life, and endured
it only by imagining the intolerable. In his agitation
there was the equivalent of an explosion that tore
him apart but suffocated him nevertheless.

Cornelius van Haarlem: *Venus and Adonis*.

Gemäldegalerie, Brunswick.

33. They had erected the guillotine in the prison garden.

Titian: *Venus.*

Uffizi, Florence.

Note that this is the (ideal) model for Manet's *Olympia*. Cf. p 149.

Titian: Ariadne asleep, from the *Bacchanalia*. The curious attitude of the child has rarely been noted.

Prado, Madrid.

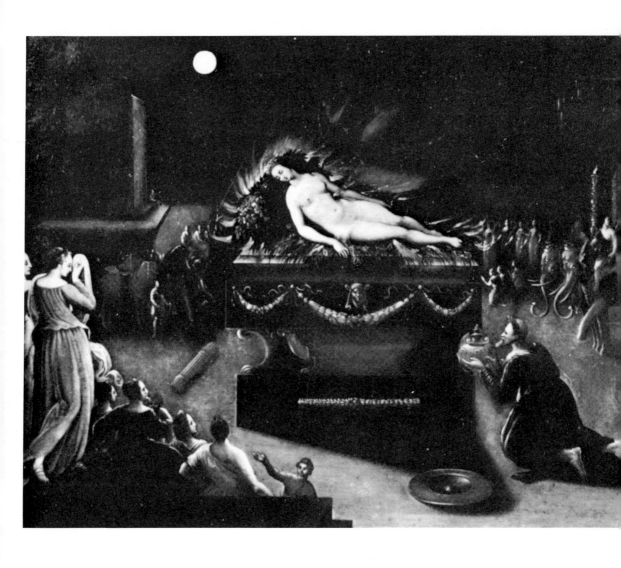

Antoine-Caron: *The Apotheosis of Semele.*

Tintoretto: *Vulcan Surprises Mars and Venus.*

Munich.

Tintoretto: *Judith and Holofernes.*

Prado, Madrid.

Vermeer of Delft: *The Sweethearts.*

Gemäldegalerie, Dresden.

117

Anonymous seventeenth century Flemish: *Saint John the Baptist* (detail).

Prado, Madrid.

Poussin: *The Couple and the Voyeur.*

Louvre.

"Poussin's erotic obsession, which in theory runs counter to his classicism, apparently came to nothing. . . . If he betrayed himself, it was above all in an unused sketch."

Poussin: Hermaphrodite (engraving by Bernard Picard fils).

Bibliothèque Nationale.

Rembrandt: *Joseph and Potiphar's Wife* (1634).

Rembrandt: *The Alcove* (1637).

Bibliothèque Nationale.

Rubens: *Medusa*.

Gemäldegalerie, Vienna.

122

Rubens: *The Horrors of War*
(sketch).

Coll. Chevrier.

Rubens: *The Consequences of*
War.

Pitti, Florence.

Boucher: *Pastoral Lover.* Painting
commissioned by Louis XV. *Right:
The Test of Love.*

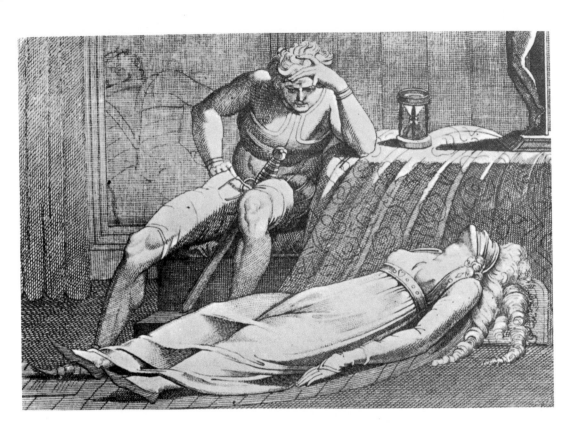

Henry Füseli (1741–1825):
Open Heart . . .

Bibliothèque Nationale. Cf. *The Drawings of Henry Füseli*, New York, 1949.

Füseli: *The Witches* (Macbeth).

Engraving by Barathier, 1813. Bibliothèque Nationale.

Füseli: *The Nightmare.*

Engraving by Laurede. Bibliothèque
Nationale.

Goya: *The Old Women.*

Musée de Lille.

5. GOYA

The problem opened up by the solitary sadness of Sade cannot be resolved through a tiresome effort that does no more than put words into play. Only in humor is an answer given to the ultimate question of human life. The only way to respond to the possibility of overcoming horror is in a rush of the blood. Each time, the response takes the form of a sudden leap into humor, and it means nothing but just this leap into humor. I could probably have extracted from Sade's language a move toward violence (though Sade's last years lead one to believe that, as death approached, he was seized by a sinister weariness).[34]

34. See G. Bataille, *Erotism*, pp. 170–173.

Goya: *Nude Maja*.

Goya: *Tantalus (The Capri-chos)*.

Goya: *Love and Death.*

Bibliothèque Nationale.

The question does not juxtapose one justifiable way of seeing with another, unjustifiable way. It juxtaposes contradictory nervous conditions, which can ultimately only be treated by sedatives or tonics.

The question is still a hauntingly painful one. Only one possibility remains: to set an example of furious rage against one of depressed horror. Sade and Goya lived at about the same time.[35] Sade,

Goya: *Matrimonial Madness.*

Bibliothèque Nationale.

35. Goya was born six years after Sade, in Spain, and died in France fourteen years after him. Goya was struck by complete deafness in Bordeaux in 1792.

locked up in his prisons, sometimes at the extreme edge of madness; Goya, deaf for thirty-six years, locked up in a prison of absolute deafness. The French Revolution awakened hope in both of them: both men had a pathological loathing of any regime founded on religion. But more than anything else, an obsession with excessive pain unites them. Goya, unlike Sade, did not associate pain with sensuous pleasure. However, his obsession with death and pain contained a convulsive violence that approximates to eroticism. But eroticism is in a sense an outlet, an infamous outlet for horror. Goya's nightmare,

Goya: *The Flagellators.*

San Fernando, Madrid.

Goya: *The Cannibals* (1).

Musée de Besançon.

like his deafness, imprisoned him, making it humanly impossible to say whether Sade or Goya had been more cruelly imprisoned by fate. There is no doubt that even in his aberration Sade had human feelings. As for Goya, he reached total aberration in his engravings, his drawings, and his paintings (without, it is true, breaking any laws); and more-

over, it may be that on the whole Sade remained within the limits of these laws.[36]

36. However, he only took to satisfying himself in imagination, through writing, in prison and at a late stage. Nowadays, the affair in Marseilles, which undoubtedly led to his being imprisoned for life, would not have such grave consequences.

Goya: *The Cannibals* (2).

Musée de Besançon.

Goya: *The Beheading.*

Coll. Villagonzalo. Cf. René
Huyghe, *Dialogue avec le visible*, Paris,
1955.

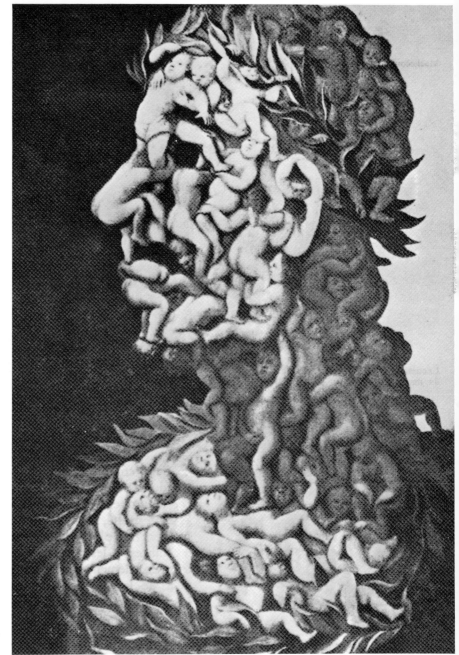

Arcimboldo: *Portrait of Herod.*

Coll. Cardazzo, Venice.

Painting formerly belonging to the Liechtensteins, at the time when Prince Karl (1563–1627) was viceroy of Bohemia.

Machecoul: the chateau of Gilles de Rais.

Lacoste (Vaucluse): the chateau of the Marquis de Sade. Cf. pp. 111.

6. GILLES DE RAIS AND ERZSEBET BATHORY

Sade knew of Gilles de Rais, and appreciated in this man a hardness of stone. This hardness is what is most remarkable: "When the children finally lay dead, he would kiss them . . . and choosing among them the most handsome ones with the finest limbs, he would set them aside to be admired and have their bodies cruelly opened up, relishing the sight of their inner organs." These words deprive me forever of the possibility of not trembling: "And very

often . . . when the children were dying, he would sit on their stomachs and take pleasure in seeing them die this way, and he *would laugh about it* with [his servants] Corrillaut and Henriet. . . ." Ultimately, the sire de Rais, who had drunk to excess in order to maximize his excitement, would fall over in a heap. The servants cleaned up the room, washed away the blood . . . , and while the master slept, they took care to burn the items of clothing one by one, wanting, they said, to avoid the "bad smells."[37]

If he had known of the existence of Erzsébet Báthory, there is not the slightest doubt that Sade would have felt the fiercest exaltation. What he knew of Isabeau de Bavière sent him into raptures; Erzsébet Báthory would have made him howl like a wild beast. I say it in this book; and I can do so only

Erzébet Báthory and her chateau.

37. Cf. *Procès de Gilles de Rais.* Documents with an introduction by G. Bataille: Club français du Livre, 1959.

under the emblem of tears. I write these desolate phrases in a state of mind quite the opposite of the delirious sangfroid that the name Erzsébet Báthory calls up. It is not a question of remorse, nor of a rage of desire as it was in Sade's mind. It concerns opening consciousness to the representation of what man really is. Faced with this representation, Christianity went into hiding. Beyond a doubt, mankind as a whole must forever remain in hiding, but human consciousness—in pride and humility, with passion and in trembling—must be open to the zenith of horror. Although Sade can be read with ease today, it has not changed the number of crimes—even sadistic crimes—but it fully opens human nature to a consciousness of itself.

Géricault: *Leda* (1).

P. P. Prud'hon: Frontispiece to *Phrosine et Mélidore,* in the *Oeuvres* of P. J. Bernard, 1797.

Etching by Prud'hon, finished by Roger with a burin.

7. THE EVOLUTION OF THE MODERN WORLD

Clearly, consciousness is the only issue. This book, for its author, has only one meaning: *it opens up consciousness of the self!*

The period that followed Sade and Goya lost this aspect of shock. It marked a summit that no one has reached since. It would be premature, though, to say that human nature had finally become more gentle. Subsequent wars have given no proof of this. . . . It nonetheless remains true that, from Gilles de Rais, who never stated his principles, to the Marquis de Sade, who stated his but never really put them into action, we see a decline in violence. In his fortresses, Gilles de Rais tortured and killed dozens of children, perhaps even hundreds. A little more than a century later, under cover of the walls of her chateaus in Hungary, a highborn lady, Erzsébet Báthory, put to death her young maidservants, and later on young girls of nobility. This she did with infinite cruelty. The nineteenth century was in principle less

violent. True, the wars of the twentieth century gave the impression of an increase of unleashed fury. But however immense the horror may have been, this furious violence was measured: it was an ignominy perfected through discipline!

The cruelty of intensified war and a suffocating discipline reduced the element of lawless release and relief that war had formerly accorded to the victors. Conversely, added to the slaughter was the rotting horror, the sinking horror of the camps. Horror resolutely acquired a sense of depression: the wars of our century have mechanized war, war has become senile. The world finally gives in to reason. Even in war, work becomes the guiding principle, its fundamental law.

Delacroix: *Woman in Stockings.*

Louvre.

144

Delacroix: *Odalisque au perroquet.*

Musée de Lyon.

Delacroix: *The Death of Sar-
danapalus* (pp. 147, 148:
details).

Louvre.

But to the extent that work turns away from violence, it gains in consciousness what it loses in blind
brutality. This new orientation came to be mirrored
in painting especially. Painting escapes idealistic
stagnation. Even though it takes liberties with regard to exactitude and to the real world, it wants
above all to destroy idealism. It could be that in one

Delacroix

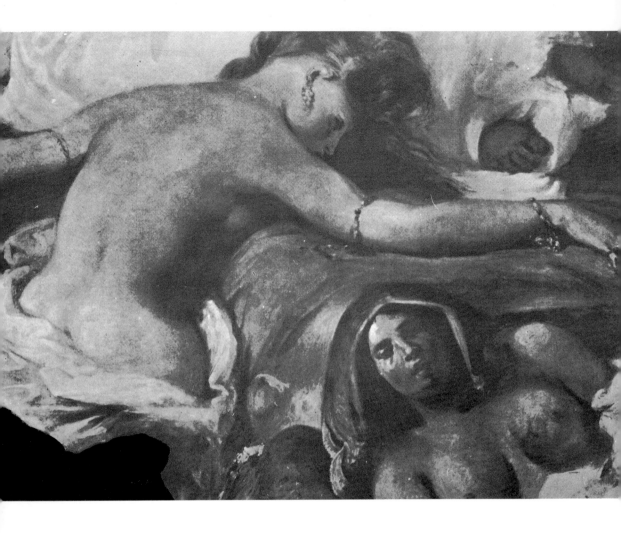

Delacroix

sense eroticism runs counter to work. But this opposition is in no way vital. What threatens man today is not material pleasure at all. In principle, material pleasure conflicts with the accumulation of wealth. But the accumulation of wealth—at least in part—is injurious to the pleasure we are entitled to expect from it. The accumulation of wealth leads to overproduction, whose only possible outcome is war. I am not saying that eroticism is the only remedy against the threat of poverty, linked to the unreasonable accumulation of wealth. Far from it. But unless we consider the various possibilities for consumption which are opposed to war, and for which erotic pleasure—the instant consumption of energy—is the model, we will never discover an outlet founded on reason.

Manet: *Olympia* (etching).

Bibliothèque Nationale.

Cézanne: *The Orgy* (1864–1868).

Private collection, Paris.

Cf. Maurice Raynal, *Cézanne,* Skira, 1954. This work belongs to the painter's "Veronese" period.

Cézanne: *A Modern Olympia*
(1872–1873?).

8. DELACROIX, MANET, DEGAS, GUSTAVE MOREAU AND THE SURREALISTS

Degas: *La Maison Tellier.*

Bibliothèque Nationale, Estampes.

From here on, painting had the sense of an open possibility going, in one sense, further than literature. Not further than Sade—but for many years

Sade was not well known: only the privileged were able to read the few copies of his work in circulation.

Even though Delacroix, on the whole, remained faithful to the principles of idealistic painting, he shifted in the direction of a new kind of painting and on the level of eroticism he linked his painting to the representation of death.

Degas: *La Maison Tellier.*

Monotypes made for Ambroise Vollard's edition of the works of Maupassant.

Toulouse-Lautrec: *The Two Friends.*

154

Musée d'Albi.

Toulouse-Lautrec: *Abandon.*

Coll. Prof. Schnitz, Zurich.

155

Gustave Moreau: *Tattooed Salome.*

Musée Gustave Moreau, Paris.

Manet was the first to break decisively with the principles of conventional painting, representing what he saw rather than what he was supposed to see. This decision led him in the direction of raw vision, a brutal vision that convention had not deformed. Manet's nudes have a brusqueness never veiled by the clothes of custom, which depresses, nor the cloth of convention, which suppresses. The same goes for the girls in the brothels as depicted in Degas' monotypes, where this incongruity is underscored.[39]

Clearly, Gustave Moreau's paintings take the opposite direction. Everything in them is conventional. Only their violence is contrary to convention: Delacroix's violence was so great that the conventional in his paintings scarcely conceals the forms that follow the principles of idealism. It was not violence, but perversion and sexual obsession that linked the figures of Gustave Moreau to the anguishing nudity of eroticism.

I must now speak, in concluding, about surrealist painting, which in short represents the mannerism of today. Mannerism? This word no longer carries any sense of disparagement in the minds of those who use it. I have recourse to the word only in the sense that it interprets a tensed violence, without which we could never free ourselves from convention. I want to use it to express the violence of Delacroix or of Manet, or the fever of Gustave Moreau. I use it in order to emphasize an opposition to classi-

39. The young Cézanne is imbued with the same tendency: his *Olympia* was intended to differ from Manet's through a marked incongruity, but it is, on the whole, no more convincing than the one by Manet (who found more truth, more strangeness, in his response to the intensity of sexual attraction).

Gustave Moreau: *Delilah.*

Coll. Robert Lebel, Paris.

Gustave Moreau: *The Apparition.*

Odilon Redon: *The Heart Has Its Reasons* . . .

Petit Palais, Paris.

Renoir: Frontispiece for *Pages de Mallarmé* (1891).

Van Gogh: Nude.

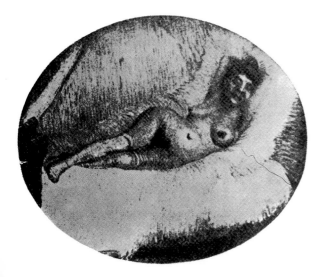

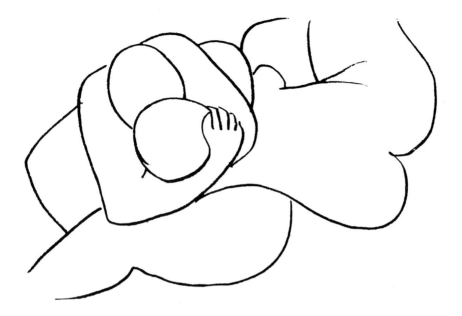

cism, which is always in quest of unchanging truths: mannerism is the quest for fever!

This quest, it is true, could serve as a pretext for the need, itself an unhealthy one, to attract attention: such is the case with someone who would deceive with eroticism, forgetting its dangerous truth.[40]

Today, no one restricts the word surrealism to the school that André Breton wanted to claim under this name. I prefer however to speak of mannerism; I want to indicate a fundamental unity between painters whose obsession it is to interpret fever: fever, desire, burning passion. I pay no heed to the artifice the word mannerism suggests: if the word is linked to desire, it is in the minds of those who desire an excess of feeling. The essential characteristic

Matisse: *Couple.*

40. I am speaking of Salvador Dali, whose painting formerly seemed passionate to me, but in whom I see nothing today but artifice. But I think the painter allowed himself to be taken in by the at once laughable and ardent strangeness of his artifice.

of the painters of whom I speak is a hatred of convention. This alone made them love the heat of eroticism—I mean the unbreathable heat given off by eroticism. Essentially, the painting I refer to boils over, it is alive . . . it burns . . . I cannot speak of it with the coolness required of judgments and classifications.

Picasso: *Faun Unveiling a Nymph* (1930–1936).

Watercolor for the *Vollard suite*, 1937.

BY WAY OF CONCLUSION

1. COMPELLING FIGURES

In the preceding two chapters I wished to bring out how an unbounded eroticism passed smoothly into conscious eroticism.

Does this passage from the unrestrained violence of war to the representation of tragedy convey a sense of decline?

Would combat—for the human condition—take on the importance of tragedy? The question is ultimately an agonizing one.

The initial impulse is to dismiss the importance of comedy.

A feeling of degradation depresses us if we set calculation against unleashed passion, against fearlessness.

As we know, however, the richness of such a possibility is not so easily attained. Like vengeance—a dish always eaten cold—the dazzled but clear consciousness of our riches desires the abatement of violence, the relative coolness of the passions. Man reaches the height of his potential in two steps. The first is to let go, but the second is to become aware. We have to evaluate what it is we lose in becoming conscious, but first we must realize that within the limits of this humanity that imprisons us, clearness of consciousness means a cooling off. Linked with consciousness, we calculate the inevitable fall. The following principle is no less true: we cannot differentiate between human and conscious.

That which is not conscious is not human.

III

Pablo Ruiz Picasso was born in Malaga in 1881. From 1901 he lived in France. (Georges Ribémont-Dessaignes has written of him: "Nothing that one can say of Picasso is accurate.") But we might say that Gomez de la Serna has named him "Toreador of painting." From his early childhood, indeed, he lived in the atmosphere of bullfights (Cf. Roland Penrose, *Picasso, His Life and Work,* London, 1958), and the corrida retained a central place in his life (as is witnessed in his drawings, as well as in Jean Desvilles's film, *Picasso, romancero du Picador*).

Picasso: *Picador and Girl.*

Galerie Louise Leiris.

Picasso: *The Couple.*

Galerie Louise Leiris.

We must make room for this first necessity. We cannot exist, we cannot live humanely except through the meanderings of time: the totality of time alone makes up and completes human life. Consciousness at its origin is fragile—because of the violence of the passions; it comes to light a little later on because of their attenuation. We cannot scorn violence, nor can we laugh at its remission.

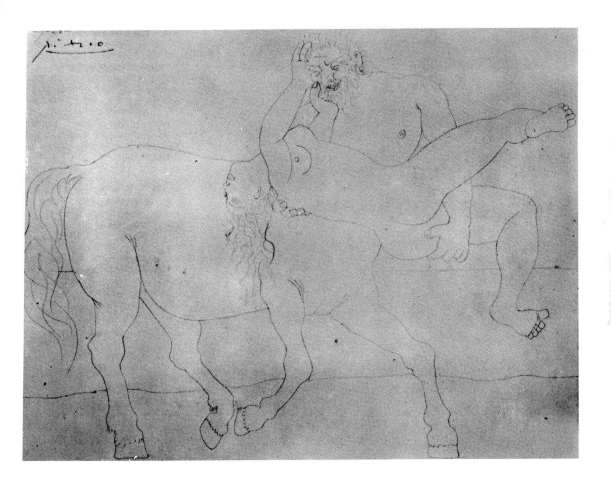

Can the meaning of a precise moment appear all at once? It need hardly be pointed out: only the succession of moments can become clear. One moment has meaning only in its relation to other moments. We are at each instant only fragments deprived of meaning if we do not relate these fragments to other fragments. How can we refer to this completed whole?

Picasso: *The Centaur Nessus* (silver point, 1920).

Galerie Louise Leiris.

Max Ernst, born in 1891 in Brühl, Rhenania, began painting before the war. After the armistice, he took part in the Dada movement, which originated in Zurich in 1916. From 1920 onward he exhibited his work in Paris, having moved there in 1922. He took part in the creation of the Surrealist movement in 1924. Living in France, he had great difficulty leaving the country for America in 1941. He stayed in America until 1949. In 1946 he married the American Dorothea Tanning, also a painter. In 1954 he won the Venice Biennial prize, which brought both his glory and his exclusion from the Surrealist group (which gradually fell apart through the exclusion of a number of painters who continue to be important within surrealism).

Cf. Max Ernst: *Beyond Painting,* New York, 1948. (This book also contains a bibliography by Bernard Karpel.) *Max Ernst* (a catalogue compiled by Gabriel Vienne, preface by Jean Cassou, bibliographical note by M.E.), Paris, 1959. (Catalogue of the Retrospective Exposition of 1959.) Patrick Waldberg, *Max Ernst,* J. J. Pauvert, Paris, 1958.

Jean Desvilles, *Une Semaine de bonté ou les sept éléments capitaux* (1961), film based on the novel by Max Ernst.

Cf. *Dictionnaire de Sexologie,* J. J. Pauvert, Paris, 1962.

Max Ernst: *The Daughers of Lot.*

Coll. Mrs. Doris Starrels, Los Angeles.

Max Ernst: *Messaline Child.*

Cf. Patrick Waldberg: *Max Ernst,*
J. J. Pauvert, Paris, 1958.

André Masson: *Massacre*
(1933).

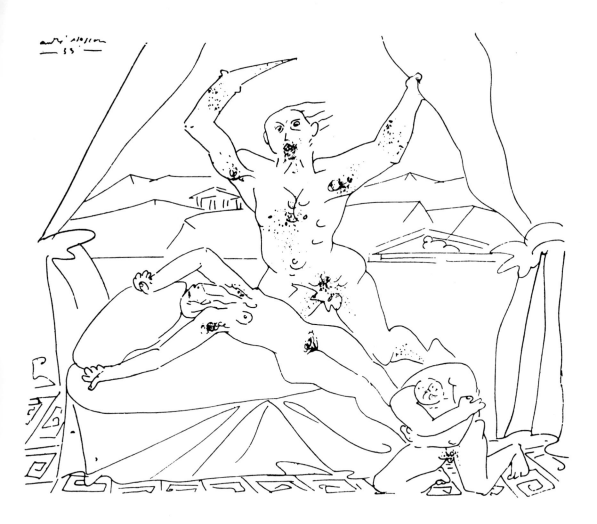

André Masson was born in 1896 in Balagny, Ile-de-France. He studied painting first at the Académie Royale in Brussels, then at the Ecole des Beaux-Arts in Paris. He took part in the war as a soldier in the infantry. "He returned deeply affected by this experience, both physically and nervously." "It is from the period immediately after the war that date Masson's first erotic drawings and watercolors, the free expression of that love of life which . . . always underlies his works." André Masson's imposing eroticism has many affinities with that of William Blake. Masson was a fervent admirer of Sade. Under the significant title of "Erotic Land," Masson held an exhibition of drawings at the Galerie Vendôme in 1948. Masson is without doubt one of the best exponents of the profound and troubling religious depths of erotism.

Cf. "Elément pour une biographie," by Michel Leiris, in *André Masson,* a collective work by friends of the painter, published 15 April, 1940.

Cf. also: Pascal Pia: *André Masson,* N.R.F., 1930, and Michel Leiris and Georges Limbour, *André Masson et son oeuvre,* Geneva, 1947.

André Masson: *Armchair for Pauline Borghese.*

André Masson: *Praying Mantis.*

Galerie Louise Leiris.

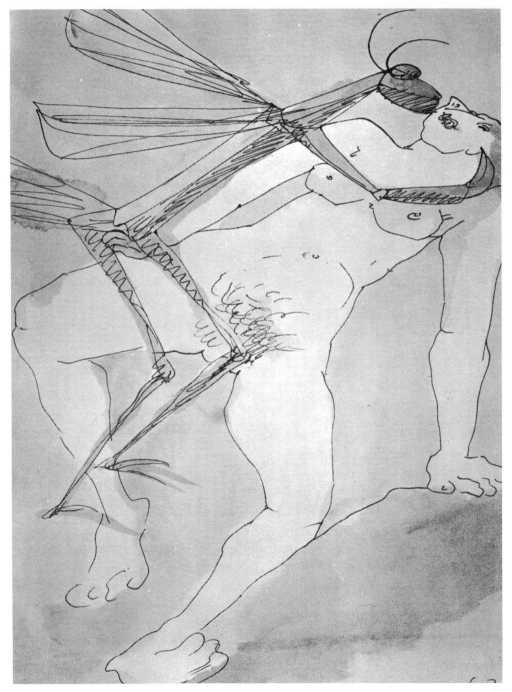

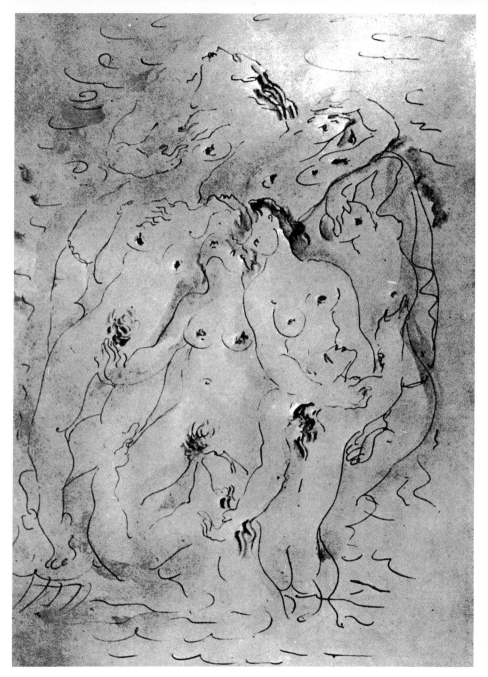

André Masson: *Damned Women* (1922).

Galerie Louis Leiris.

All I can do for now is to add a new view, and, if possible, the final view, to those I have already proposed.

This would be to plunge into a complete whole whose cohesion might appear to me at long last.

The principle of this movement is the impossibility of a clear consciousness that would be conscious only of its immediate experience.

André   Masson: *Lesbos* (1922).

Galerie Louis Leiris.

Paul Delvaux: *The Lunar
City* (1944).

Coll. Alex Salkin, New York.

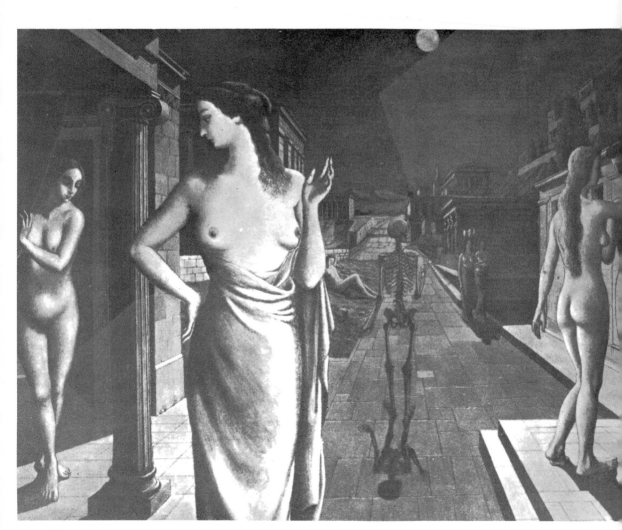

Paul Delvaux was born in 1897 in Antheit, Belgium. After a brief period, "he developed in a direction that paralleled Surrealism, without becoming a part of it." Between 1939 and 1944, two trips to Italy led to new experiments with color and perspective. In 1945, Henri Stock made a film about Paul Delvaux, based on a scenario by René Micha, with a commentary by Paul Eluard.

Cf. Henri Stock: *Le Monde de Paul Delvaux* [film], 1945. Claude Spaak, *Paul Delvaux,* (in French and Flemish), Antwerp, 1948. [Paul Eluard], *Paul Delvaux,* ed. René Drouin, Paris, 1948.

Paul Delvaux: *The Pink Knots* (1936).

Coll. Claude Spaak, Paris.

Paul Delvaux: *Night Train* (1947).

René Magritte was born in Les-
sines, Belgium, in 1898. In 1926,
along with a certain number of
Belgian friends, he supported Surrealism, which expressed the profound meaning of his painting,
which is poetry. If his erotism is
soveriegn, it is to the extent that it
is poetry. Erotism cannot be entire-
ly revealed without poetry.

René Magritte: *Olympia*
(1947).

Hans Bellmer: *Doll.*

Cf. H. Bellmer: *Les yeux de la poupée,*
illustrated with texts by Paul Éluard,
a work compiled between 1936 and
1938, completed and published in
1949 in Paris. H. Bellmer, *21 reproductions 1939–1950,* Paris, 1950.

Cf. *Dictionnaire de Sexologie,* J. J. Pauvert, Paris, 1962.

*The night shines forth in its way, from
the eyes to the heart. The night annuls
the sensuous, the only pure space.*
 —Paul Eluard

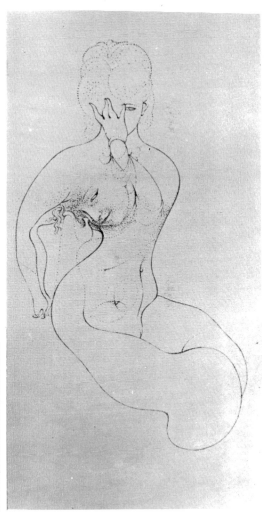

Two drawings by Hans Bellmer.

Cf. "Anatomy of the Image," in *Le
Terrain vague,* 1957.

Hans Bellmer: *To Sade* (New York, 1947).

Balthus (nickname of Balthazar Klossowski) was born in Paris in 1908. He received considerable recognition with his first exhibition in 1934. Called up in 1939, he was wounded in the early days of the war in Alsace. Balthus's paintings are few in number and, although he is to be counted among the most "modern" of painters, nothing clearly distinguishes them from those of traditional painters. Until recently, Balthus was director of the Villa Medici in Rome.

Balthus: *The Room* (1952–1954).

Galerie Henriette Gomes, Paris.

Balthus: *The Dream* (1955–
1956).

Galerie Henriette Gomes, Paris.

Leonor Fini was born of an Argentian father and a Swiss mother. Their ancestors were Spanish, Venetian, Slavic, German and Neapolitan.

Cf. Marcel Brion, *Leonor Fini et son oeuvre*, J. J. Pauvert, Paris, 1955.

Of Leonor Fini, Jean Genet writes (*Lettre à Léonor Fini,* Paris, 1950): "Would I be so impassioned by a work if I had not discovered in it, and in its very form, not that toward which I am headed—and which will belong to me alone—but these same desperate elements scattered across funereal splendours?"

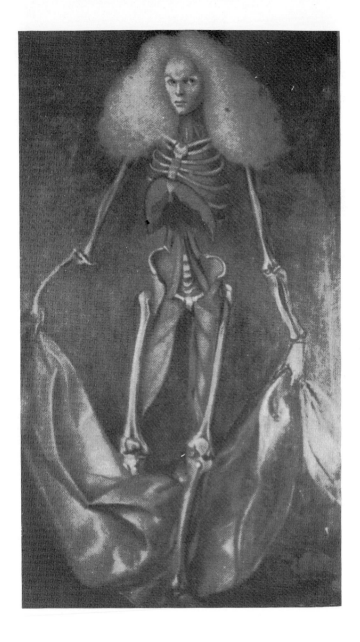

Leonor Fini: *The Angel of Anatomy* (1950).

(First stage of the painting.)

Leonor Fini: *The Room* (1941).

I propose in my reflections to dwell upon some fairly unknown contemporaries, whom I know only through photographs. The two people in question had little consciousness of the moments they were living. The first is a voodoo *sacrificer.* The second is a victim of Chinese torture, a torture that obviously could have no other outcome than death.

The game I am setting up for myself is to represent what they were living at the moment the lens fixed their image on the glass or on the film.

Leonor Fini: *Friendship* (1957).

Cf. Ornelia Volta: *Le Vampire, la mort, le sang, la peur,* J. J. Pauvert, Paris, 1962.

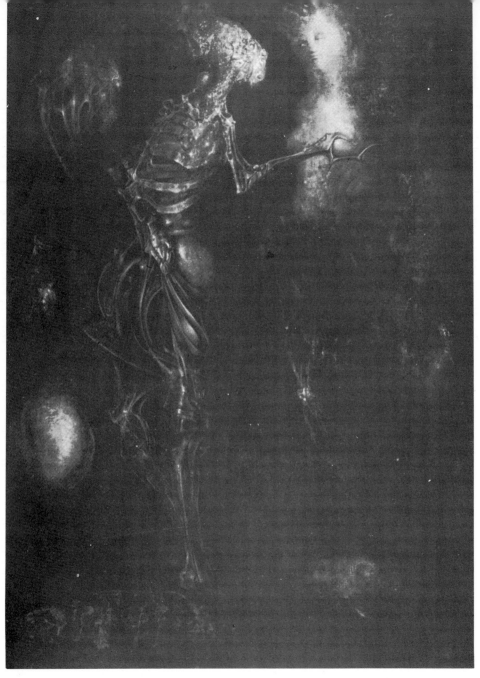

Leonor Fini: *Unconditional Love* (1959).

Francis Bacon, a young English painter and among the most important of his generation, is becoming known through his unusual paintings marked by their brusque character.

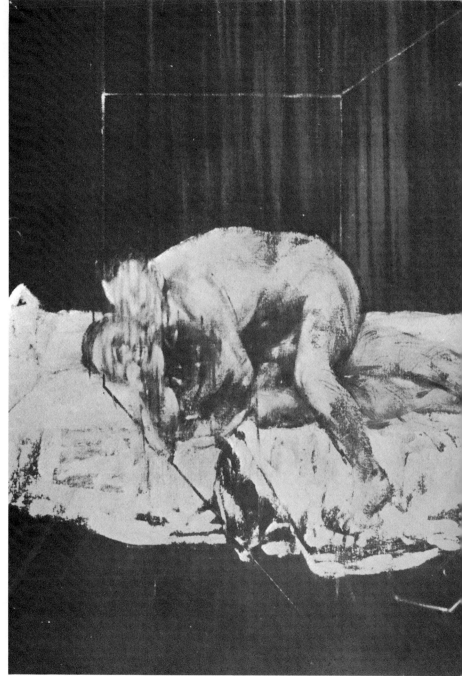

Francis Bacon: *The Room.*

Hanover Gallery, London.

Félix Labisse was born in 1905 in Douai. From 1927 he lived in Paris and on the Belgian coast (Ostende, Le Zoute). From 1931 he made sets and costumes for the theater. In 1947 he was the subject of a film that Alain Renais shot in the artist's atelier.

Cf. *Félix Labisse,* Documents compiled by Nane Bettex-Cailler, Geneva, 1958. *Félix Labisse,* Brussels, 1960.

Félix Labisse: *The Prodigal Daughter* (1943).

Dorothea Tanning: *Sleeping Woman* (1953).

Dorothea Tanning: *Voltage*

Dorothea Tanning was born in Galesburg (Illinois); after an apparently traditional period (in the way Balthus's art is "traditional"), her painting attained a profound abstractness that holds intact its fundamental eroticism.

Félix Labisse: *Poetic Morning* (1944). From the left: Sade (seen from the back), Jean-Louis Barrault, Jarry, William Blake, Apollinaire, Labisse, Picasso, Robert Desnos.

Coll. Jean Baure.

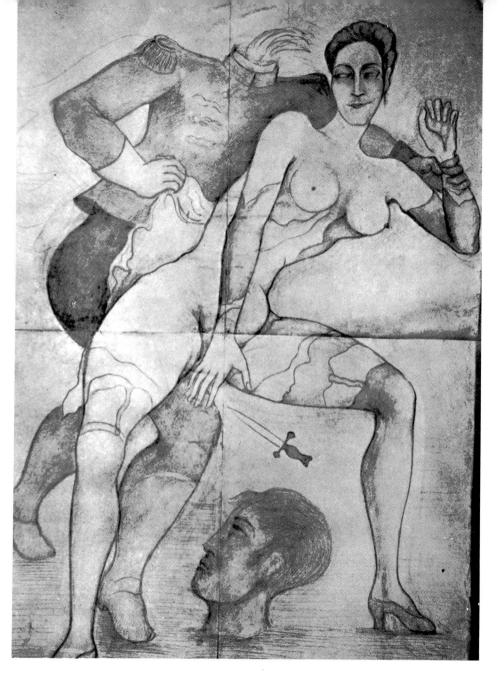

Pierre Klossowski: *Roberte and the Colossus* (variant).

Pierre Klossowski, born in Paris in 1905, is the older brother of Balthus (cf. p. 181). He is known above all as a writer (*Sade, mon prochain,* Ed. du Seuil, Paris, 1947; *La vocation suspendue,* novel, Gallimard, Paris, 1947; *Roberte ce soir,* Minuit, Paris, 1953; *Le Bain de Diane,* J. J. Pauvert, Paris, 1956; *La Révocation de l'Edit de Nantes,* Minuit, Paris, 1959; *Le Souffleur, ou Le Théâtre de société,* novel, J. J. Pauvert, Paris, 1960).

Pierre Klossowski: *Diane and Acetaeon.*

Pierre Klossowski: Drawing
for *Roberte ce soir.*

Pierre Klossowski: Drawing
for *Roberte ce soir.*

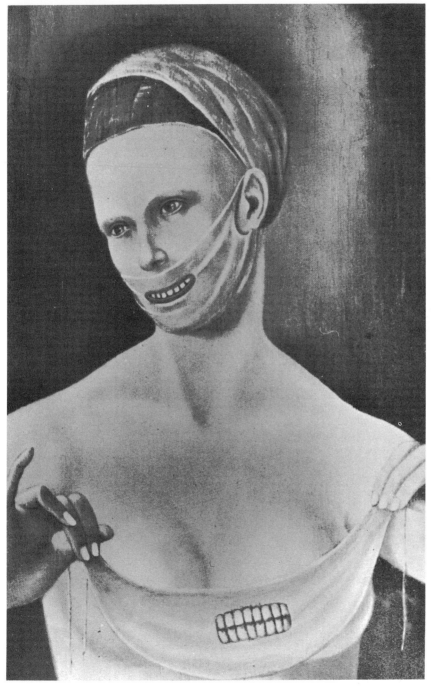

Lepri: *The Mouth and the Truth* (1955).

Cf. Alain Jouffroy: *La chambre noire de Lepri*, Ed. della Conchiglia, Milan, 1956.

Clovis Trouille: *The Tomb* (formerly: de Sade).

Clovis Trouille: *First Class.*

Clovis Trouille, born in Aisne in 1889, became one of the strangest painters of his generation. He worked for a long time in a factory that supplied wax dummies to the Musée Grévin. Cf. *Dictionnaire de Sexologie,* J. J. Pauvert, Paris, 1962, and Lo Duca, *Préface au Catalogue de l'Exposition Clovis Trouille,* Galerie Raymond Cordier, Paris, 1963.

2. VOODOO SACRIFICE

What the voodoo sacrificer experienced was a kind of ecstasy. An ecstasy comparable in a way to drunkenness. An ecstasy brought about by the killing of birds. I will add nothing to these very beautiful photographs, which we owe to one of today's most remarkable and renowned photographers, except to say that to look at them with passion is to penetrate a world as far away as possible from our own.

This world is one of blood sacrifice.

Across time, the blood sacrifice opened man's eyes to the contemplation of the vexing reality, completely outside daily reality, which is given in the religious world this strange name: the *sacred*. We can give no justifiable definition of this word. But some of us can still imagine (try to imagine) what *sacred* means. And no doubt such readers of this book, faced with these photographs, will try to relate this meaning to the image of what the bloody reality of the sacrifice represents to them, the bloody reality of the animal's death in the sacrifice. To the image, and perhaps to the troubled feeling where a vertiginous horror and drunkenness come together, where the reality of death itself, of the sudden coming of death, holds a meaning heavier than life, heavier—and more glacial.

These are photographs of the voodoo ceremonial as it is practiced today in certain regions of America, where it developed among black slaves. An accurate and vivid description of the religion of these Americans, originally from Africa, is to be found in a very beautiful work by Alfred Métraux, one of the finest ethnographers of our time (*Le Vaudoo,* Gallimard, Paris, 1955). All the more vivid since the author, in order to know it better, himself became an initiate.

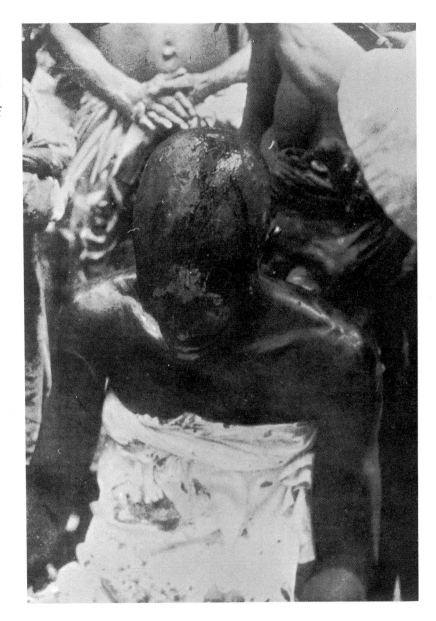

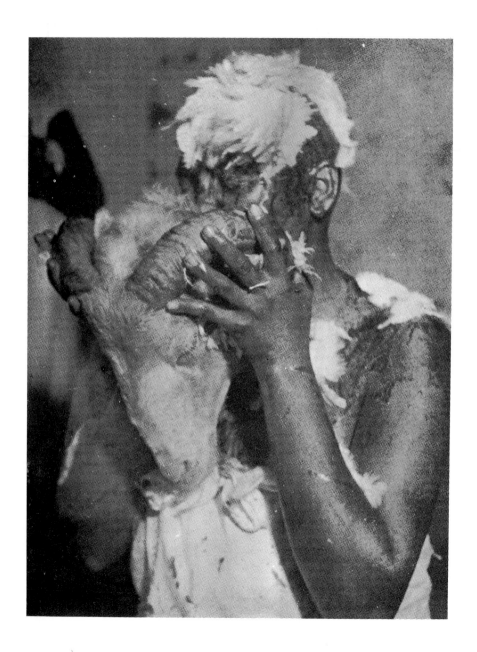

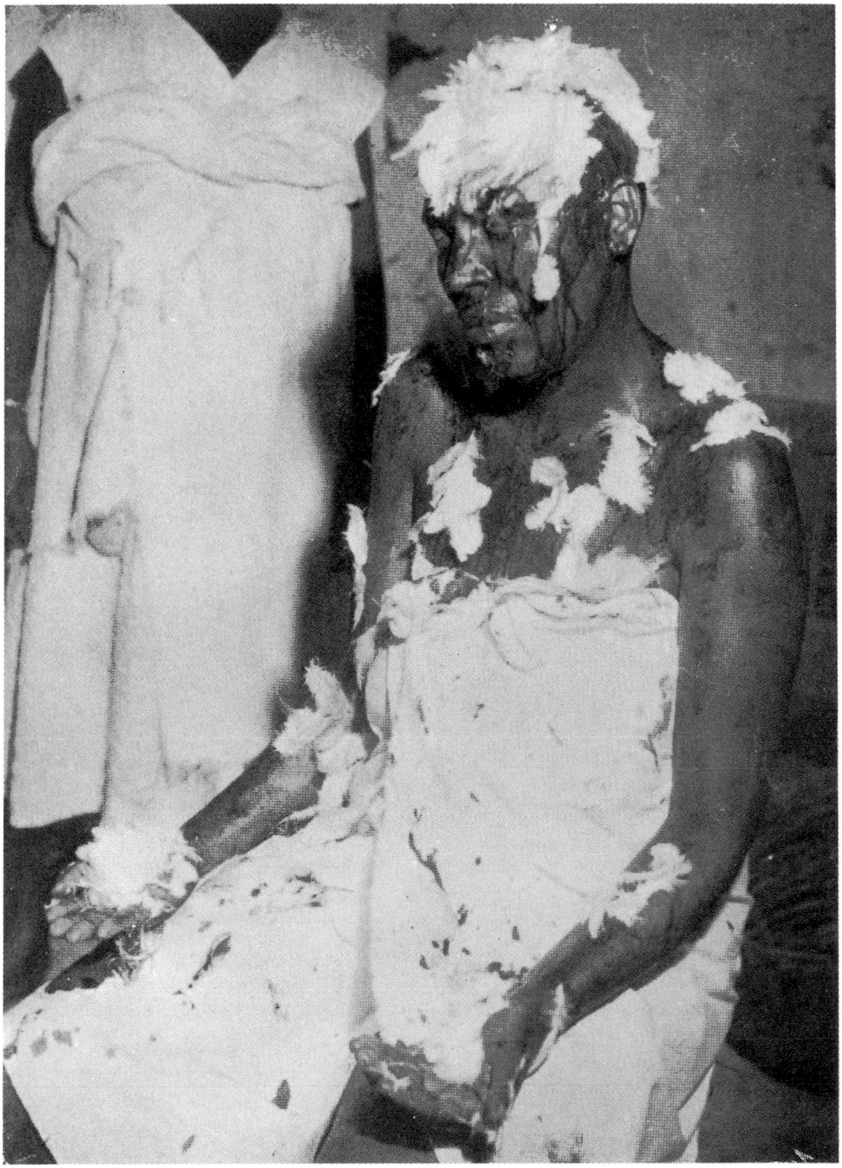

These shots were published in part by Dumas and by Carpeaux. Carpeaux claims to have witnessed the torture on April 10th, 1905. On March 25th, 1905, the "Cheng-Pao" published the following imperial decree: "The Mongolian Princes demand that the aforesaid Fou-Tchou-Li, guilty of the murder of Prince Ao-Han-Ouan, be burned alive, but the Emperor finds this torture too cruel and condemns Fou-Tchou-Li to slow death by *Leng-Tch'e* (cutting into pieces). Respect this!" This torture dates from the Manchu dynasty (1644–1911).

Cf. Georges Dumas: *Traité de psychologie,* Paris, 1923, and Louis Carpeaux, *Pékin qui s'en va,* ed. A. Maloine, Paris, 1913.

3. CHINESE TORTURE

The world evoked by this straightforward image of a tortured man, photographed several times during the torture, in Peking, is, to my knowledge, the most anguishing of worlds accessible to us through images captured on film. The torture shown here is that of the *Hundred Pieces,* reserved for the gravest of crimes. One of these shots was reproduced in 1923 in Georges Dumas's *Traité de psychologie.* But the author attributes it incorrectly to a much earlier date and speaks of it as an example of *horripilation:* when one's hair stands on end! I have been told that in order to prolong the torture, opium is administered to the condemned man. Dumas insists upon the ecstatic appearance of the victim's expression. There is, of course, something undeniable in his expression, no doubt due at least in part to the opium, which augments what is most anguishing about this photograph. Since 1925, I have owned one of these pictures (reproduced on p. 204). It was given to me by Dr. Borel, one of the first French psychoanalysts.

This photograph had a decisive role in my life. I have never stopped being obsessed by this image of pain, at once ecstatic(?) and intolerable. I wonder what the Marquis de Sade would have thought of this image, Sade who dreamed of torture, which was inaccessible to him, but who never witnessed an actual torture session. In one way or another, this image was incessantly before his eyes. But Sade would have wished to see it in solitude, at least in relative solitude, without which the ecstatic and voluptuous effect is inconceivable.

Much later, in 1938, a friend initiated me into the practice of yoga. It was on this occasion that I discerned, in the violence of this image, an infinite capacity for reversal. Through this violence—even today I cannot imagine a more insane, more shocking form—I was so stunned that I reached the point of ecstasy. My purpose is to illustrate a fundamental connection between religious ecstasy and eroticism—and in particular sadism. From the most unspeakable to the most elevated. This book is not written from within the limited experience of most men.

I cannot doubt it.

What I suddenly saw, and what imprisoned me in anguish—but which at the same time delivered me from it—was the identity of these perfect contraries, divine ecstasy and its opposite, extreme horror.

And this is my inevitable conclusion to a history of eroticism. But I should add: limited to its own domain, eroticism could never have achieved this fundamental truth divulged in *religious eroticism,* the identity of horror and the religious. Religion in its entirety was founded upon sacrifice. But only an interminable detour allows us to reach that instant where the contraries seem visibly conjoined, where the religious horror disclosed in sacrifice becomes linked to the abyss of eroticism, to the last shuddering tears that eroticism alone can illuminate.

Aztec human sacrifice, around 1500.

Codex Vaticanus 3738, folio no. 54.

A tradition of horror . . . (see following pages)

After the Aztec sacrifices,
the violence of the Conquest.

Cf. John Everhardts Cloppenburg:
*Le Miroir de la Tyrannie Espagnole Per-
petrée aux Indes Occidentales,* Amster-
dam, 1620.

"Certain artists have expressed sa-
domasochistic tendencies in painting the martyrdom of Christians or
similar scenes; the determining influence of underlying sadistic tendencies that in fact first led them to
seek out such scenes. . . ." Cf. E.
Pesch: *La psychologie affective,* Paris,
1947.

The botched attempt: "Ja-
cob, Duke of Monmouth,
has his head cut off." Engraving by Jan Luiken,
1711.

Coll. Henry Kahnweiler.

"A woman loses her seven sons." Engraving by Jan Luiken (1711).

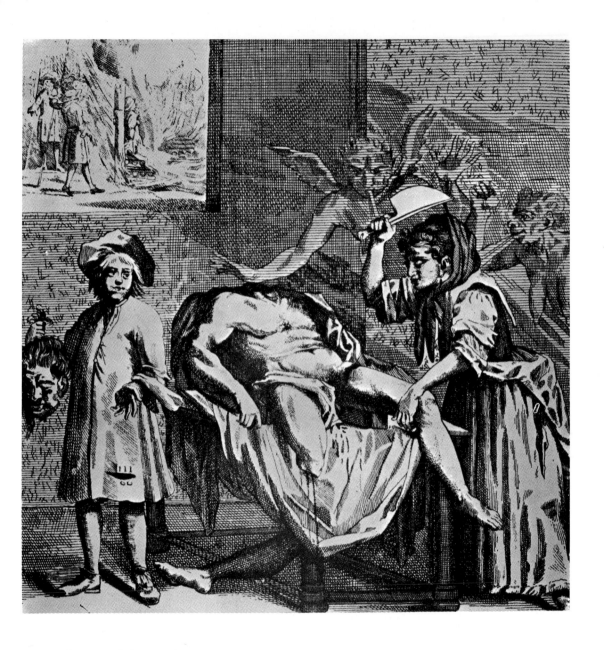

Excesses of Love, English engraving
(Mary Aubrey).

Bibliothèque Nationale.

Horror and eroticism . . . Yi Dam and his Çakti. Tibetan art.

Cf. Maurice: "Eritis sicut dii," *Minotaure,* no. 11.
André Malraux: *Les voix du silence,* Paris, 1951, p. 495.

Musée Guimet.

Photo Raoul Ubac.

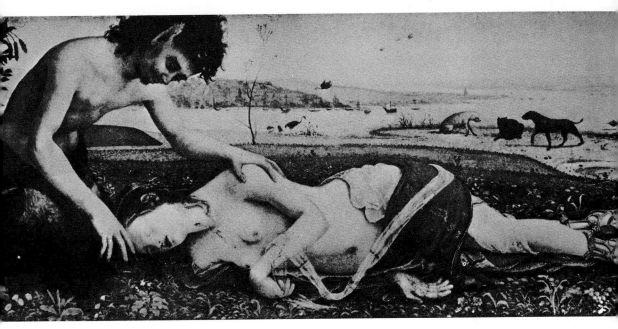

Piero di Cosimo: *The Death of Procris.*

National Gallery, London.

CITY LIGHTS PUBLICATIONS

Angulo de, Jaime and Gui. JAIME IN TAOS
Antler. FACTORY
Artaud, Antonin. ARTAUD ANTHOLOGY
Bataille, Georges. THE TEARS OF EROS
Bataille, Georges. EROTISM: Death and Sensuality
Bataille, Georges. STORY OF THE EYE
Baudelaire, Charles. TWENTY PROSE POEMS
Baudelaire, Charles. INTIMATE JOURNALS
Bowles, Paul. A HUNDRED CAMELS IN THE COURTYARD
Breá, Juan. RED SPANISH NOTEBOOK
Brecht, Stefan. POEMS
Broughton, James. SEEING THE LIGHT
Buckley, Lord. HIPARAMA OF THE CLASSICS
Buhle, Paul, ed. FREE SPIRITS
Bukowski, Charles. THE MOST BEAUTIFUL WOMAN IN TOWN
Bukowski, Charles. TALES OF ORDINARY MADNESS
Bukowski, Charles. NOTES OF A DIRTY OLD MAN
Burroughs, William S. THE BURROUGHS FILE
Burroughs, William S. THE YAGE LETTERS
Cardenal, Ernesto. FROM NICARAGUA, WITH LOVE
Carrington, Leonora. THE HEARING TRUMPET
Cassady, Neal. THE FIRST THIRD
Choukri, Mohamed. FOR BREAD ALONE
CITY LIGHTS REVIEW #1
CITY LIGHTS REVIEW #2
CITY LIGHTS REVIEW #3
Cocteau, Jean. THE WHITE BOOK (LE LIVRE BLANC)
Codrescu, Andrei, ed. EXQUISITE CORPSE READER
Cornford, Adam. ANIMATIONS
Corso, Gregory. GASOLINE
David-Neel, Alexandra. SECRET ORAL TEACHINGS IN
    TIBETAN BUDDHIST SECTS
Deleuze, Gilles. SPINOZA: PRACTICAL PHILOSOPHY
Dick, Leslie. WITHOUT FALLING
Di Prima, Diane. REVOLUTIONARY LETTERS
Di Prima, Diane. PIECES OF A SONG
Doolittle, Hilda (H.D.) NOTES ON THOUGHT & VISION
Ducornet, Rikki. ENTERING FIRE
Duras, Marguerite. DURAS BY DURAS

Eberhardt, Isabelle. THE OBLIVION SEEKERS
Fenollosa, Ernest. THE CHINESE WRITTEN
    CHARACTER AS A MEDIUM FOR POETRY
Ferlinghetti, Lawrence. LEAVES OF LIFE
Ferlinghetti, Lawrence. PICTURES OF THE GONE WORLD
Ferlinghetti, Lawrence. SEVEN DAYS IN NICARAGUA LIBRE
García Lorca, Federico. ODE TO WALT WHITMAN &
    OTHER POEMS
García Lorca, Federico. POEM OF THE DEEP SONG
Gascoyne, David. A SHORT SURVEY OF SURREALISM
Ginsberg, Allen. HOWL & OTHER POEMS
Ginsberg, Allen. KADDISH & OTHER POEMS
Ginsberg, Allen. REALITY SANDWICHES
Ginsberg, Allen. PLANET NEWS
Ginsberg, Allen. THE FALL OF AMERICA
Ginsberg, Allen. MIND BREATHS
Ginsberg, Allen. PLUTONIAN ODE
Ginsberg, Allen. IRON HORSE
Ginsberg, Allen. INDIAN JOURNALS
Ginsberg, Allen. SCENES ALONG THE ROAD
Goethe, J. W. von. TALES FOR TRANSFORMATION
Hayton-Keeva, Sally, ed. VALIANT WOMEN IN WAR & EXILE
Herron, Don. THE LITERARY WORLD OF SAN FRANCISCO
Higman, Perry, ed. LOVE POEMS FROM SPAIN
    AND SPANISH AMERICA
Kerouac, Jack. BOOK OF DREAMS
Kerouac, Jack. SCATTERED POEMS
Kovic, Ron. AROUND THE WORLD IN 8 DAYS
La Duke, Betty. COMPANERAS: Women, Art & Social
    Change in Latin America
La Loca. ADVENTURES ON THE ISLE OF ADOLESCENCE
Lamantia, Philip. MEADOWLARK WEST
Lamantia, Philip. BECOMING VISIBLE
Laughlin, James. THE MASTER OF THOSE WHO KNOW
Laughlin, James. SELECTED POEMS: 1935-1985
Lowry, Malcolm. SELECTED POEMS
Ludlow, Fitz Hugh. THE HASHEESH EATER
Marcelin, Philippe-Thoby. THE BEAST OF THE HAITIAN
    HILLS
Masereel, Frans. PASSIONATE JOURNEY
McDonough, Kaye. ZELDA
Moore, Daniel. BURNT HEART

Mrabet, Mohammed. THE BOY WHO SET THE FIRE
Mrabet, Mohammed. THE LEMON
Mrabet, Mohammed. LOVE WITH A FEW HAIRS
Mrabet, Mohammed. M'HASHISH
Murguia, Alejandro, ed. VOLCAN: Poems from Central America
O'Hara, Frank. LUNCH POEMS
Olson, Charles. CALL ME ISHMAEL
Orlovsky, Peter. CLEAN A POEMS
Paschke, Barbara, ed. CLAMOR OF INNOCENCE: Stories
    from Central America
Pessoa, Fernando. ALWAYS ASTONISHED: Selected Prose
Pasolini, Pier Paolo. ROMAN POEMS
Poe, Edgar Alan. THE UNKNOWN POE
Porta, Antonio. KISSES FROM ANOTHER DREAM
Purdy, James. GARMENTS THE LIVING WEAR
Purdy, James. IN A SHALLOW GRAVE
Prévert, Jacques. PAROLES
Rey-Rosa, Rodrigo. THE BEGGAR'S KNIFE
Rigaud, Milo. SECRETS OF VOODOO
Saadawi El, Nawal. MEMOIRS OF A WOMAN DOCTOR
Sawyer-Lauçanno, Christopher, transl. THE DESTRUCTION OF THE
    JAGUAR: Poems from the Books of Chilam Balam
Sclauzero, Mariarosa. MARLENE
Serge, Victor. RESISTANCE
Shepard, Sam. MOTEL CHRONICLES
Shepard, Sam. FOOL FOR LOVE & THE SAD LAMENT
    OF PECOS BILL
Smith, Michael. IT A COME
Snyder, Gary. THE OLD WAYS
Tutuola, Amos. FEATHER WOMAN OF THE JUNGLE
Tutuola, Amos. SIMBI & THE SATYR OF THE DARK JUNGLE
Waley, Arthur. THE NINE SONGS
Wilson, Colin. POETRY AND MYSTICISM